Lord Dufferin

The Tenure of Land in Ireland

Lord Dufferin

The Tenure of Land in Ireland

ISBN/EAN: 9783337324858

Printed in Europe, USA, Canada, Australia, Japan

Cover: Foto ©ninafisch / pixelio.de

More available books at **www.hansebooks.com**

THE

TENURE OF LAND

IN

IRELAND.

ABRIDGED FROM THE WORK

OF

THE RIGHT HON. LORD DUFFERIN, K.P.,

ON THAT SUBJECT;

WITH ADDITIONS AND ALTERATIONS.

DUBLIN:

JOHN FALCONER, 53, UPPER SACKVILLE-STREET,

PRINTER TO HER MAJESTY'S STATIONERY OFFICE.

1870.

PREFACE.

THE following pages contain the substance of Lord Dufferin's work on "Irish Emigration and the Tenure of Land in Ireland."

The opinions propounded in that volume seem so just and sound—supported as they are by a mass of evidence taken under the authority of a Parliamentary Commission, by statements of able writers, eminent statisticians and political economists, and by the experience of practical men connected with Irish land—the reasoning is so cogent, and the spirit in which the subject is discussed is so liberal and candid—while the positions of the author, though assailed, have been so little displaced—that it has been deemed desirable at this crisis, when the consideration of the land tenure of Ireland by Parliament is inevitably impending, to reproduce these opinions and arguments in a size and at a price that will make them accessible to the general public of the empire.

The text of Lord Dufferin has, for the most part, been preserved, though not professedly as his. Such changes, by way of addition, omission, or qualification, have alone been made, as were required by the lapse of time since the publication of the work, by the condensation of statements, and by the omission of the evidence to sustain these statements, which was given at great length in notes. Wherever it could conveniently be done, this evidence is briefly incorporated with the text; those who desire fuller information on the point are referred to the work itself.

This task has not been undertaken without the permission of Lord Dufferin, but he is in nowise answerable for the manner in which his volume has been dealt with.

TENURE OF LAND IN IRELAND.

CHAPTER I.

IRISH EMIGRATION.—IS IT A CALAMITY?

IT is not too much to say that the subject of transcendent interest at the present time is that of the Land Tenure of Ireland. Commissioners, under the authority of the State, and Commissioners appointed by the leading organs of public opinion, have investigated the relations between the owners and occupants of land in that country. Statesmen have endeavoured to deal with these relations in the legislature; public men, from the highest to the lowest, have discussed them in the press; and the Parliament to assemble in 1870 will have to deal with the subject without delay.

That much error, much prejudice, and not a little injustice, have found their way into these discussions is not surprising, and is, even to a great extent, consistent with honesty of purpose and a desire to be truthful. In any country it is difficult to disentangle the threads of popular sentiment, or to follow out the intricate operation of economic laws. But in Ireland a hundred influences—many of them compatible with the purest patriotism and the most scrupulous integrity—have contrived to prejudice local opinion and to mislead the national conscience. Added to this is the natural habit of the mind to look at a subject mainly, if not altogether, from a special point of view, and to deal with it accordingly. But the true statesman must regard the subject from every point, and must endeavour to protect, so far as is possible, the interests and rights of all—not to promote the welfare of one class by acting unjustly towards another. We may be sure that any scheme is radically faulty which violates the great fundamental principles of Liberty, Justice, and Government.

The advocates of the popular side of the question of Land Tenure have brought numerous charges against landlords and land-laws—some put forward by men supposed to speak with the highest authority—and in terms not always dignified or temperate. It is proposed to specify these charges, and examine them in the following pages.

Stripped of all exaggerated phraseology the accusations with which the landlords are assailed may be condensed into the following series of propositions:—

1. That the emigration from Ireland has been a curse to that country.

2. That this emigration has been occasioned by the eviction of the rural population by their landlords.

3. That acts of eviction in Ireland are to be attributed rather to the cruelty and injustice of the landlords than to any failure on the part of those evicted to fulfil their legitimate obligations.

4. That the present discontent in Ireland has been chiefly occasioned by the iniquity of the laws affecting the tenure of land.

5. That a change in those laws in a specified direction would pacify discontent and create agricultural prosperity.

Are these things true? That is the inquiry it is proposed to prosecute.

First—Has the Irish exodus, as it has been termed, been a calamity or the reverse?

We have to consider this question from two points of view, inasmuch as it has affected the condition of two classes of persons, namely, those who went away, and those who stayed at home.

There is one single fact which will probably be accepted as a safe indication of the effects of emigration on the destinies of those who took part in it. To their honour, within 17 years after their departure they had sent back to Ireland upwards of £13,000,000 of money,[*] chiefly for the purpose of enabling their friends to follow their example. Now, unless they had prospered, these savings could not have been accumulated; unless their new existence had been full of promise they would not have tempted their brethren to join them. But what if, instead of setting forth to reap the golden harvests of the West, these forlorn multitudes had remained pent up within their rainy valleys, would the existing population, those that have clung to the old country in spite of everything—would they be now the better or the worse? Two obvious consequences must have followed—wages would have been lower, rents higher than they are now, while a very large proportion of the

---

[*] See Report of the Government Emigration Board, 1865.

peasantry would be occupying farms half the size of those they are at present cultivating. Now, low wages and high rents may be advantageous in a certain sense to the manufacturer, to the landlord, and to the recruiting sergeant; but how do they affect the masses—the tenant, the labourer, and the mechanic?

In the west of Ireland some 20 years ago the rate of agricultural wages varied from half-a-crown to five shillings a week. Ever since it has gradually advanced—in some places it has doubled—in others it has more than doubled. In the North the farm servant has become almost master of the market, and is certainly better off than many of the small tenants; in the South, though still not paid as he should be, his position is much improved, while, all over the country, the navvy, the quarryman, and the drainer are receiving from 10s. to 12s. a week.

Occasionally complaints are being made of a dearth of hands: it is true this outcry generally means that at particular seasons of pressure farmers can no longer turn into their fields at a moment's notice the crowd of ill-paid cottiers that used to wait their pleasure in enforced idleness during the slack seasons of the year. But any temporary inconvenience of this kind will be more than counterbalanced by the necessity which will be imposed on the landed interest, whether proprietors or tenants, to guarantee to those they wish to retain in their service comfortable lodging, fair remuneration, and above all, permanent employment. It is this growing difficulty of obtaining an unlimited amount of *casual* labour at low rates during summer that is weaning the embarrassed tenant from his yearning after land. Eventually those only will be able to engage in farming with advantage who can either reduce their need of the labourer to a minimum, or can afford to pay him good wages all the year round. Hitherto the agricultural class has been composed too exclusively of occupiers, who though able to perform the ordinary operations required on their farms during two-thirds of the year, were dependent at seed time and harvest on a half-employed labouring population, who were relegated to idleness and penury, the moment the grain was sown or stored. A worse distribution of industry could not be imagined. What we want are fewer indigent occupiers and more constant employment for the labourer; for it is quite evident that an area cultivated by 10 farmers and 15 farm servants in constant work, would be better managed than if it were subdivided amongst 15 farmers who gave only occasional employment to 15 labourers.

To those who closely watch the transitional phases of our national life, it is very evident that the foregoing and other cognate agencies are gradually emancipating the farming classes from the tyranny of competition. During the last few years many a struggling tenant has been tempted by the rise of wages to hand his farm over to his more competent neighbour, and himself to pass from a life of precarious husbandry into the disciplined ranks of labour, where his industry is both better remunerated, and employed to a better purpose than ever it was before: and in proportion as the peasant becomes aware of the existence of a more hopeful theatre for his industry, whether at home or abroad, than that presented to him and his children by the miserable patch he miserably cultivates, that morbid hunger for a bit of land which has been the bane of Ireland will gradually subside; competition will relax something of its suicidal energy; and in the same way as the Irish labourer has already risen from the condition of a serf to an equality of comfort with his employer, will the tenant farmer, relieved from the lateral pressure of his superfluous associates, be able to treat with his landlord on more independent terms.

But it may be objected by those who deplore emigration, that had these vanished thousands remained among us, production would have been stimulated, and the well-being of the whole community proportionately increased. Let us see how far this would be a reasonable expectation.

Had no emigration taken place from Ireland, and had the population continued to multiply at its normal rate, the additional increase to our present numbers would by this time have amounted to three millions of souls, and as there is no reason to suppose that such a circumstance would have materially expanded the restricted manufacturing operations of the country, the larger proportion·of these three millions would have had to depend upon the land for their support. Now, it appears from an official Report, drawn up on the conjoint authority of Archbishop Whately, Archbishop Murray, and Mr. More O'Farrell, that in 1846 five persons were employed in the cultivation of the soil of Ireland for every two that cultivated the same quantity of land in Great Britain, while the agricultural produce of Great Britain was four times the agricultural produce of Ireland. As a matter of fact, therefore, so far as the past is concerned, the addition to the agricultural produce of Ireland has not been proportionate to the excess of the agricultural population.

It may, however, be pretended that so unsatisfactory a result is to be accounted for by the unintelligent method in which this redundancy of labour has been applied to the soil. But in the Lothians of Scotland, and in certain parts of England, the art of agriculture is neither unintelligently nor unsuccessfully practised, and probably a given space is there made to produce as remunerative a crop as the united efforts of man and nature are destined to accomplish; yet in those localities it has been found that about 18 men, with a small proportion of women, are sufficient to cultivate in the most efficient manner 500 acres of arable land.

Were we to apply this proportion to the 15,832,892 acres of land, under cattle and crops in Ireland, we shall see that some half million of persons would be able to cultivate the entire area. But by the census return of 1861 the number of adult males engaged in agricultural pursuits in that country is considerably over a million. Consequently, notwithstanding the emigration which has taken place, the disproportion between the respective amounts of agricultural labour, and the area cultivated in the two countries, which was noted in 1846 by Archbishop Murray and his colleagues as being in the ratio of 5 to 2, may still be taken as about 2 to 1. If we compare the number of hands employed in the cultivation of specified areas in those parts of England and Scotland where agriculture is best understood with the number on the occupied area of Ireland, even supposing that the whole, instead of one-third, was tillage land, it will probably be found that at the date of our last census, some three hundred thousand persons were engaged in the cultivation of the soil in excess of those whose exertions, if directed with greater skill and energy, and accompanied by an adequate expenditure of capital, would be sufficient to ensure us as high a rate of production as is obtained in the sister country.*

---

* From a comparative table of the proportion of cultivators to the extent of land under tillage and pasture in Belgium, Flanders, England, and Ireland, as well as in the four provinces, and some of the counties of the latter kingdom, together with the amount of produce obtained from corresponding areas in each locality, it appears that the same amount of labour which is found sufficient in England to cultivate $11\frac{1}{4}$ acres in a highly efficient manner is employed in Ireland in the less perfect cultivation of 6 acres. In other words, whereas in Ireland it takes four men to raise 15 tons of grain off 24 acres, in England only two are required to raise 16 tons off 23 acres.

It is urged, however, that it is unfair to argue that because great economy of labour is practicable on the large farms of England, a similar rule can be applied to the small subdivisions of Ireland. If this were indeed the case, it would be an admission very damaging to the advocates of the small farm system; but though in some respects there may be a saving of labour, over extensive areas, as compared with very diminished

Consequently, even making allowance for the decrease of the agricultural population which has since been going on, it is probable that there is still in Ireland a considerable section of the inhabitants with their wives and children dependent for their support upon the land, whose misapplied industry is as unproductive as if it were devoted to the grinding of a treadmill or the lifting of shot; but though contributing nothing to the producing power of the class with which they are incorporated, they have to be supported out of its profits, of which they diminish by so much the share to the remainder.

But it is urged that if only the Belgian system could be introduced into Ireland, our present agricultural population would be anything but in excess of the requirements of the country's husbandry.

Assuming, which is not the fact, that the Belgian system of agriculture (the minute garden husbandry of East Flanders) not only is possible, but applicable to the present circumstances of Ireland, reference to statistical tables will show that, at all events, in many parts of Ireland, if not in all, the proportion of the agricultural population to the area it occupies is almost as dense as it is in Belgium. If, therefore, the Belgian system is to be introduced, and our tenant farmers are to take to growing tobacco, hops, onions, colza, and carrots, on patches of three or four acres, in the expectation of making a fortune, emigration cannot be accused of having deprived them of the opportunity.

But in Belgium it is only by dint of the most unremitting industry, and a traditional skill, which has been the growth of centuries, by a vast expenditure of capital, and by the application

ones, the necessary difference will be found far less than is supposed ;—within certain limits, economy of labour, though not of buildings or of machinery, is as practicable on reasonably small farms as on large. If a proof were wanting, we need only again refer to the table, when we shall see that the tillage lands of Ulster and Leinster, the two provinces from which the largest rate of produce per acre is obtained, are cultivated by a fewer number of hands than are crowded into the husbandry of Munster and Connaught, and that in Down and Antrim, the two Irish counties in which agriculture is supposed to be most advanced, and the average size of the farms smaller than elsewhere, the proportion of cultivators to the acre is considerably less than it is in Cork and Kerry. In fact, the density of the agricultural population over the several areas referred to appears to be in an inverse ratio to the rate of their agricultural produce ; and no matter how the calculation is conducted, or what districts are brought into comparison, whether England with Ireland, Ulster with Connaught, or Down with Cork, the same conclusion is evolved, viz. : that in those districts which are worse cultivated, a far larger number of persons are engaged in agriculture than are necessary to obtain the same results as are arrived at in those districts which are better cultivated.

of enormous quantities of manure, that the agricultural class, whose rate of increase is slow, and whose redundant members a flourishing manufacturing industry is ready to absorb, has been able, under peculiar advantages of climate, situation, and markets, to maintain an existence at all times considerably straitened, and daily becoming more difficult under the pressure of increasing competition. In Ireland these fostering conditions are as yet completely wanting, and years may elapse before they are created. How can we be justified then, in the expectation of so remote a contingency, in tethering down to the soil by artificial means, an agricultural population far in excess of the requirements and the system of husbandry best adapted to the present circumstances of the country, in the expectation of the ultimate introduction of a system of "petite culture," which, even then, would hardly afford adequate employment to our existing numbers.

But that the system is inapplicable to Ireland is admitted upon evidence above all exception. In 1866 Lord Dufferin and five other witnesses, Judge Longfield, Mr. Dillon, Mr. M'Carthy Downing, Mr. Curling, and the Roman Catholic Bishop of Cloyne, were examined before Mr. Maguire's Land Tenure Committee. No one will pretend that the sympathies of those five gentlemen were unduly enlisted on the landlord's side. Some of them were members of the National Association, and their bias—so far as their minds were susceptible of bias—was clearly in favour of the tenant.

All were asked the same question. What is the smallest area which a tenant can cultivate with advantage, or over which you would extend the protection of a lease? And none of them considered that a tenant could live comfortably upon or improve a farm of less than from 15 to 20 acres.

Even the latter when pressed to name the *minimum* area on which a farmer could live, admits that "small farms, with any amount of industry must be precarious," and that a tenant to be comfortable ought to have "20 acres or *upwards;*" If reason and not passion is to guide us, it must be conceded that a greater amount of intelligent energy than necessary is dissipated in the cultivation of land. At all events, if the champions of the tenant's cause are themselves found condemning small holdings and 15-acre leaseholds as unprofitable and "*precarious,*" and if it is shown that the extinction of farms in Ireland has been hitherto almost entirely confined to that category, may not the landlords be absolved from the charge of undue consolidation?

Let us now examine the agricultural system of Belgium, to which reference is often made. Fortunately, in the work of M. De Laveleye, we possess a text book on the subject, of European celebrity.

According to popular belief Belgium is cultivated by a peasant proprietary twice as numerous in proportion to the area they occupy as the agricultural population of Ireland, living in peculiarly easy circumstances, and affording unmistakable evidence of the advantages of *la petite culture*. The real facts are these:—That, making a proportionate deduction for the population employed on the pasture lands of both countries, the total population dependent on tillage in Ireland is probably almost as dense as that of Belgium. That the greater portion of Belgium is cultivated, not by small proprietors, but by tenants (and almost entirely so wherever *la petite culture* is carried to excess). That the competition for land is intense, and rack-rents universal. That from 1830 to 1846 rents have risen 25 per cent., and between 1846 and 1860 40 per cent., though the price of grain has only risen 5 per cent. The leases are rarely granted for a term exceeding nine years, and frequently for only three or five years. That the average profits of the farmer are scarcely more than three per cent., instead of from 7 to 10 per cent., as in England. That the condition of the agricultural population is worst where the subdivision of farms is greatest, and best where the farms are largest. That the Belgian labourer is supposed to be the most industrious and the worst paid of any labourer in Europe, that the farmer is scarcely better off than the labourer; and that in Flanders population is not merely at a standstill, but diminishing.

It may be objected that, however little advantages to the agricultural classes themselves, *la petite culture* of Belgium turns out a greater amount of gross produce than any other method of cultivation known in Europe. This is probably the case, if we omit all reference to cost, and, under suitable circumstances, it is (at all events, for the landlord) a most profitable system. But the provinces of Belgium where *la petite culture* prevails are thickly studded with populous towns and innumerable villages, and the land around them is devoted to an extensive system of market-gardening, only practicable in such localities. The facilities for obtaining manure are exceptional, and high manuring at a cost of from £10 to £18 to the acre, stolen crops,* together with the cultivation of plants

---

* That is, turnips, spurrey, flax, early potatoes, carrots, and some other plants.

used in the adjacent manufactories, are the keystones of Belgian agriculture. In a great number of instances where the plots of land are very diminutive the farm is only auxiliary to its occupier's trade, just as the little holdings in Antrim or Down are auxiliary to the hand-loom weaving of Ulster. And, lastly, both in respect of climate, in the forcing power of the sun (without which stolen crops are very precarious), and in variety of plants for which a ready sale can be obtained, Belgium has advantages in which parts of Great Britain and nearly all Ireland are deficient. To expect, therefore, that because holdings of three, four or five acres can be cultivated with advantage around a cluster of large Belgian towns, and amid the densest population in Europe, of which the agricultural class forms less than one half, a similar system can be introduced into Ireland, with its rainy, sunless climate, its sparse urban population, its restricted markets, and its limited manufactures, seems as unreasonable as to argue that because it pays Mr. Early Pease, of Brompton, to employ a press of hands and £50 of manure per acre in raising asparagus for Covent-garden market, a similar expenditure and a similar method of cultivation should be adopted in the valleys of Wales and the straths of the Highlands.

The chief lesson which we may learn from Flemish husbandry is this—that a very high rate of production is compatible with low wages, rack-rents, and exceptionally short leases; and that diminutive tenancies, under certain favourable conditions, may be profitable to the proprietor while they are disadvantageous to the tenant.

But if, instead of the reduced numbers at present left in this false position, the hundreds of thousands who have emigrated had remained at home to breed and stagnate on the overburdened soil, is it not evident that a state of things would now exist in Ireland such as no man can think of without a shudder? We do not wish, however, to imply that the existing surplus of agricultural labour, need necessarily follow their example. When once the rate of wages in a country has reached a point, which ensures to the labourer the necessaries and decencies of life, emigration ceases to be of such paramount importance, and no man could contemplate the expatriation of so many brave hearts, and strong right arms with equanimity. The true remedy for the anomaly (as was well stated in a pastoral of the Roman Catholic Archbishop of Cashel) is to be found in the development of our commercial enterprize, of our mineral resources, of our manufacturing industry. It is not

14

blood-letting to relieve a plethora, but stimulants to restore the balance of a congested circulation that are needed.

Still less would we advocate an attempt to divert, whether by moral pressure or otherwise, any portion of the land-occupying class from their present avocations. Persons of practical experience are aware that even in the most prosperous parts of Ireland the enlargement of holdings undesirably diminutive is continually taking place by a natural process, which need never involve the violent displacement of a single individual, and at a rate which rather exceeds than otherwise the accumulation of the necessary capital in the hands of those to whose farms the surrendered scraps of land are annexed. Death, bankruptcy, failing health, and the hundred casualties which diversify the current of human affairs, annually place at the disposal of the landlord a number of vacated tenancies more than sufficient to carry out any amount of judicious consolidation. To hasten, therefore, the transition which the agricultural system of Ireland is gradually undergoing, is neither his interest nor his practice. It is true the slower the absorption of the surplus agricultural labour of the country into other pursuits the worse for the general body of cultivators; but each year is improving their situation, and it is better the conviction of what is for their true advantage should penetrate their intelligence of its own accord than that their prejudices should be shocked by any extraneous influences, however well intentioned.

But to imagine that even the most scrupulous observance of this rule by every landlord in Ireland could ever have prevented, or can now check the departure of a large proportion of the people is a delusion. The increase of every nation must be limited by the extent and capabilities of the area it occupies, and the amount of capital it possesses.

This law is of universal application, though one race, from its more sordid habits or lower civilization, may be more compressible than another.

But, the appointed limits once reached, either the procreative energies of the people will be artificially restricted, as has been the case in France, or the surplus population will emigrate, as they have done from Germany, from Ireland, and to a lesser degree from England.

Up to the year 1846 the soil of Ireland retained the capacity of producing, to an almost unlimited extent, a certain root, containing all the elements necessary for the support of human life. The expansion of the population was proportionate to the facilities it enjoyed for obtaining sustenance. Suddenly, by the visitation of God, those facilities were withdrawn; the potato failed; no other product of the soil existed to take its place; corn crops neither supplied the same amount of nutriment, nor could they be grown in successive years on the same spot. The life-sustaining power of the soil had become restricted; as an inevitable consequence the population of the island has become proportionately restricted; and, exactly in the same way as the working classes of Manchester would have been obliged to remove to other centres of industry had the cotton famine continued, has the surplus population of Ireland been compelled to emigrate to a more fertile soil.

Though acting with diminished energy, the same causes may be expected for some time to come to produce similar results. The natural expansion of a prolific nation, still numbering upwards of five millions and a half, must be considerable. Did this increase maintain its normal rate, we might calculate on a net annual addition of 60,000 souls to our population; but as a large proportion of those who emigrate are men and women in their first youth, we must presume it has been considerably checked; putting, however, the excess of births over deaths at a minimum of 40,000 per annum, we shall confront a very formidable figure. How are these successive waves of fresh arrivals to be accommodated?

Even those who most deplore emigration would not recommend a resubdivision for their benefit of holdings whose size at this moment is perhaps below the desirable average: the labour market is only too amply supplied: agitation has succeeded in discouraging the introduction of English capital and in crushing everywhere, except in Ulster, our nascent manufacturing enterprise; what other alternative have you to offer, if you shut up their path across the sea? During the last six years ending with 1868 the emigration from Ireland has averaged a little over 90,000 a year; nearly one half of that emigration, therefore, has merely harmonized with the mechanical law, which only permits the introduction of water at one end of a pipe by the expulsion of a corresponding volume at the other.

In all parts of the world similar processes are occurring, and it is absurd to talk of Ireland as the only country from which an extensive emigration has proceeded. From Germany alone, and principally from the North and West of Germany, as many as

250,000 persons have emigrated in a single year; while between 1851 and 1861, even from Great Britain, the emigration has averaged as high as 71,000 a year.

Still more unreasonable is it to describe the "ruling classes" as standing alone in their opinion—an opinion most unjustly ascribed to "their stupidity and selfishness"—that emigration has been no calamity to Ireland.

To call emigration a calamity implies a confusion of ideas.

Emigration may be occasioned by a calamity: it may be followed by disastrous consequences: but it is in itself a curative process: and to confound it with the evils to which it affords relief, would be as great a blunder as to mistake the distressing accidents of suppuration for symptoms of mortification. Plans for the express purpose of stimulating emigration have been devised and advocated from time to time by such men as Mr. Smith O'Brien, Sir Thomas Wyse, Mr. Sharman Crawford, Sir George C. Lewis, and Mr. Cobden; and it would be easy to show, by numerous quotations, how common this conviction has been to every school of politics and class of society.

To attribute such a view to landlord "stupidity and selfishness" is even more gratuitous. When did a tradesman ever complain of the multitude of his customers, or a manufacturer of the easiness of the labour-market? And what is the owner of an estate other than a trader in land? His tenants are his customers; the more strenuous their competition the higher his rents, and the denser their number the more keenly will they compete; emigration has a tendency to diminish rather than to increase his rental; and if it has not done so already it is because the number of those who seek to obtain their living by the land are still out of proportion to the area capable of maintaining them.

Again, the landlord is very often a large employer of labour. "Within the last 15 years I myself," observes Lord Dufferin in 1867, "have paid away upwards of £60,000 in wages alone. During the last half of that period, in consequence of the rise in wages, I have got much less for my money than I did during the first half, and my consequent loss, comparing one period with another, would amount to several thousand pounds, and this has been a direct consequence of emigration. But, though a dealer in land, and a payer of wages, I am, above all things, an Irishman, and as an Irishman *I rejoice at any circumstance which tends to strengthen the independence of the tenant farmer, or to add to the comforts of the labourer's existence.*"

But it is said that though as yet no inconvenient diminution of the agricultural population has occurred, as is proved by the still inadequate rate of wages in the rural districts, emigration is acquiring a momentum which will carry it far beyond all reasonable limits.* This is a contingency deserving serious attention; but the first precaution to be taken is to fix those classes most exposed to the current, in a position of such comfort and stability as will enable them to resist its influence. Such an object will be far more surely promoted by whatever tends to abate the tyranny of competition than by offering those who are now hustling one another off the land any artificial inducements to continue the scramble.

Others suggest that the great works of irrigation and reclamation which still require to be executed in Ireland would more than absorb all the redundant population. To this we reply, in the first place, that during the very period which has witnessed the greatest emigration, larger areas have been reclaimed than have ever been before;† that the productive powers of the soil have been increasing in a ratio nearly corresponding to that at which the population has diminished; and that as we still have one adult cultivator to every six acres of land under crops, it is not any want of hands which hinders the island being converted into a garden from one end to the other. In the next place, the very thing to be desired is to see our surplus labour-power, now frittered away in the desultory cultivation of fields which ought to produce twice as much with one-third fewer hands, intelligently applied to the development of the country's resources. All that we contend for is, that while you are collecting your capital, and organizing your plans, for the

* "But, these things being as they are—though a judiciously conducted emigration is a most important resource for suddenly lightening the pressure of population by a single effort—and though in such an extraordinary case as that of Ireland, under the threefold operation of the potato failure, the poor law, and the general turning out of tenantry throughout the country, spontaneous emigration may at a particular crisis remove greater multitudes than it was ever proposed to remove at once by any national scheme; it still remains to be shown by experience whether a permanent stream of emigration can be kept up, sufficient to take off, as in America, all that portion of the annual increase (when proceeding at the greatest rapidity) which being in excess of the progress made during the same short period in the arts of life, tends to render living more difficult for every averagely-situated individual in the community. And unless this can be done, emigration cannot, even in an economical point of view, dispense with the necessity of checks to population."—*Mill's Polit. Economy*, p. 246.

† Between 1844 and 1862 more than 2,000,000 acres of waste land have been reclaimed.

B

introduction of that millenium of enterprise which has already disappointed the hopes of previous generations, you have no right to keep the men, whose grand-children you may perhaps eventually provide with employment, standing idle and starving in the market-place.

Notwithstanding therefore all that has been said to the contrary, we assert that not only has emigration been an infinite blessing to Ireland, but that for some years to come a considerable portion of the nation will continue to profit by its advantages. The surest means to check that emigration which compels so many noble-hearted Irishmen to leave the land of their birth, is to repress the agitation which now scares capital from her shores, and prevents the development of her industrial resources, and thus render her capable of sustaining a population far larger than any she has ever borne.

Expatriation is undoubtedly a great calamity, but emigration does not necessarily imply expatriation. Hundreds of those who go return, and if the greater number stay it is only because they prefer to do so. Nor, when Providence spread out the virgin prairies of the New World, or stored up the golden treasures of Australia, can it have been intended that attachment to the natal soil should become so predominant a passion as to deter man from taking possession of the new territories prepared for his reception. Far, then, from being in itself a calamity, emigration is an essential element in the future progress of the United Kingdom, and our fellow-countrymen who depart, even if absorbed by an alien community, often minister to our prosperity more effectually than when they dwelt amongst us. The transformation of an indigent and disaffected subject into a prosperous foreign customer is a change not wholly disadvantageous, and the industry which has gone forth to till the prairies of the West cheapens the loaf to millions in the old country.

One thing at all events is certain. In the progress of every civilized community the period must arrive when the natural increase of population overtakes the normal rate of production. The true remedy may be to communicate additional fertility to the soil; but this is seldom an immediate possibility: as a consequence the rate of increase of the population must be checked; or its standard of comfort must deteriorate; or its accruing surplus must remove. But the first necessitates an artificial and often an unnatural social system, as is said to prevail in France; and the

next is an alternative which entails the physical degradation we
have seen supervene in Ireland. There remains therefore the
third—a course in perfect harmony with the laws of nature, and
one which has already established the religion, the language, and
the freedom of England, over one-fourth of the habitable globe.
To lament the exhibition of so much enterprise, vital energy, and
colonizing power, in the race to which we belong, seems more
perverse than to stigmatize as a curse the blessing originally pronounced on those who were first bidden " to go forth and multiply
and replenish the earth."

CHAPTER II.

IRISH EMIGRATION—HAS IT BEEN CAUSED BY LANDLORDS?

SECONDLY, we now propose to examine the specific charge directed
against the landed proprietors of Ireland, viz., that the legalized
injustice of their proceedings has been the principal and active
occasion of emigration.

Many eminent persons say that such is the case. " The landlords are the cause of the emigration," is the naked and unqualified
statement which has been put forward in Parliament. " More
than a million persons have fallen victims to their injustice," is a
common assertion, and various instances of wholesale evictions are
referred to in illustration of the statement. Now, we are ready to
admit that they who make such statements believe them, but
accusations involving a large class of our fellow-countrymen in so
hateful a responsibility cannot be lightly accepted. Let us, then,
examine their validity by such tests as can be conveniently adduced.

Indeed, if we believe so much, there is a great deal more we
must believe. We must believe that all those general incentives
to emigration already enumerated, and which have told with such
effect upon England, upon Scotland, and upon Germany, have had
no influence in Ireland, although the peculiar circumstances of
Ireland were so well calculated to intensify their operation. We
must believe that the emigration from Ireland has been entirely
confined to the rural population of the country, and confined not
only to the rural population, but to less than one-half of the rural
population, viz., the occupiers of land. We must believe that the

wages of labour have doubled in 15 years—not in consequence of the emigration of the farm-servant as distinguished from the tenant-farmer, but from some other cause which has yet to be explained; and, finally, we must believe that the individuals of that class to which alone it is alleged emigration has been confined—viz., the occupiers of land—have one and all vacated their mud cabins and strips of blighted potato ground, not because they found they could no longer feed their pig or grow oats with advantage on an acre of land—not because they heard that wages were 4s. a day in New York, and that farms could be got for nothing in the Western States—not because their friends besought them to cross the Atlantic, and sent millions of money to pay their passage—but solely and entirely in consequence of their having been driven from their homes by the wanton cruelty of their landlords and the injustice of Parliament—a series of assumptions incompatible with ascertained facts.

In conducting this inquiry we shall not discuss whether the landlords of Ireland, as a class, are good men or bad men, kind or cruel. They may be as selfish, as interested, and as unscrupulous as any other men possessing the same amount of education and intelligence. But the supposed moral attributes of a particular class, or trade, or profession, cannot come within the cognizance of the politician. His only safe rule will be to take it for granted that every class, and every individual in every class, will pursue his own advantage with unflinching pertinacity; and, having meted out as justly as the clumsiness of human legislation may admit, the boundaries which are to circumscribe the respective rights of each, he must be content to accept as economically legitimate whatever does not overpass them. In all ages there have been unrelenting creditors who have insisted on their pound of flesh, but would it not be unreasonable on that account to stigmatize the recovery of debt as injustice? Unhappily, legal obligations can seldom be rendered co-extensive with moral responsibilities, and an attempt to correct an exceptional hardship in one direction, too frequently leads to the infliction of greater injuries in another.

Still less shall we notice any particular accusations of cruelty or injustice which may be alleged against individual proprietors. In the first place, they are necessarily derived from *ex parte* statements, and their merits cannot be readily investigated;* and, in the next,

---

* It is not often that an opportunity occurs of subjecting these charges to the test of an impartial inquiry, but whenever an investigation is set on foot they hardly sustain

their assistance in guiding us to an opinion on questions involving such an enormous range of observation must obviously be infinitesimal. Two of the very instances adduced during a debate in Parliament, prove the truth of this observation. For the first is the case of a landlord who turns his tenants out at midnight in winter, without previous notice, and the other tells us of a would-be purchaser of an Irish estate who was only prevented from evicting a number of cottiers by being himself hanged for murder before he had concluded his bargain. Now, as by law every tenant must receive at least eight or nine months' notice before he can be forced to surrender possession of his holding, the first case proves nothing against the laws regulating the relation of landlord and tenant, while in the second story the hero, not having been an Irish proprietor at all, can scarcely be paraded as a type of the class. No doubt many acts of harshness and cruelty have been perpetrated in Ireland, more particularly during the time of the famine. But, it is to be remembered that the famine year was an exceptional period; a sudden storm had broken out of a clear sky; the ship lay a wreck on her beam-ends. It was such a scene as reveals the mingled baseness and heroism of human nature, and doubtless, in the extremity of peril which threatened the landlords, their wives, and their children, many a man enforced his legal rights with distressing severity. That this was not the general practice is clearly stated by Judge Longfield in his evidence before Mr. Maguire's com-

strict scrutiny, a fact especially recorded in the summary of the evidence taken before the Devon Commission.

"Many of the witnesses appeared to be impressed with the idea that the power of ejectment is frequently used by landlords from caprice to strengthen their political party, or to persecute their religious opponents ; and some cases were brought before the commission as instances of that power having been so used. *But upon investigation of these cases few of them appear to justify such imputations. In general either the allegations were altogether unfounded, or mainly based upon hear-say—or it appeared that the ejectment was brought in consequence of the tenant having incurred a heavy arrear of rent, and being unwilling, or unable, to discharge it.* In many estates a small sum of money was given to those who resigned their land ; and the extent to which the increased holdings were brought was generally but small, barely sufficient for those who remained."

" There is no question that the condition of the property, as well as of the occupiers, in most of these cases, required a change, as their previous state was for the most part very miserable."—*Digest Devon Commission, Summary,* p. 830.

And again :—

" There were frequent charges made against agents of oppressive conduct, which, in general, *when investigated*, appeared merely to have consisted in compelling the payment of an arrear of rent, or *preventing a ruinous subdivision of the farms.*"—*Digest Devon Commission, Summary,* p. 1027.

mittee. In answer to a question as to whether or not a bad feeling had arisen from many proprietors in different parts of Ireland having taken steps, at the time of the famine, to consolidate their farms, he replies, " I do not think that had much to do with it; the tenants were voluntarily giving up their lands in great quantities then;" and a little further on he states that " cases of forcible eviction for the proposed consolidation were *very* few."[*] Now Judge Longfield's testimony on such a point (confirmed as it is by numerous and unimpeachable witnesses) is conclusive. He was the first and most important witness summoned before Mr. Maguire's committee. His professional position, his experience, the peculiar nature of his duties, his well-known calmness and impartiality, and above all his manifest sympathy with the cause of the tenant, invest his evidence on matters of fact with an authority that cannot be gainsaid. And it stands to reason that matters should have fallen out as Judge Longfield has described. What inducement had the poor people to stay? Their staff of life had withered in their hands and could not be replaced. A plough could hardly have turned in their potato gardens; they had neither seed, nor horses, nor even food, to carry them through the winter. No difference of tenure would have saved them. Had they owned the fee, it would have been all the same. Their only chance of life was to get away—some to the poor-house, others to America, often with the aid of the landlord, one of whom alone spent £13,000 for that purpose. As for the landlord, his position was every whit as bad. It was not a question of rent, but of existence. His lands lay around him a poisonous waste of vegetable decay, while 25s. in the pound of poor-rate was daily eating up the fee-simple of his estate. Self-interest, duty, common sense, all dictated the same course,—the enlargement of boundaries, the redistribution of farms, and the introduction of a scientific agriculture, at whatever cost of sentiment or of individual suffering. Yet with all the difficulties arising out of this state of affairs (so admirably described in the summary prefixed to the Digest of the Evidence before the Devon Commission), it is abundantly proved in evidence that, as a general rule, the inevitable changes were effected in a humane and liberal manner. Even so, the struggle too frequently proved unsuccessful, and the subsequent obliteration of nearly an entire third of the landlords of Ireland, while it associates them so conspicuously with the misfortunes of their tenants, may be accepted

[*] The same opinion was educed by the Devon Commission.

in atonement of whatever share they may have had in conniving at those remoter causes which aggravated the general calamity.

A reference to the statistics which bear upon this question will enforce the foregoing observations still more strikingly. If it is true, as is asserted, that the emigration has been principally confined to a class which cultivates the soil—the only class, in fact, which can be directly affected by the tyranny and injustice of the landed proprietor—it must necessarily follow that the number of emigrants must bear a tolerably close proportion to the number of persons who are said to have been so ruthlessly dealt with. Now the reductions of the holdings in Ireland between 1841 and the present is, of course, the measure of the limits within which the consolidation of farms has been effected and evictions have been possible. But it so happens that the total number of holdings in Ireland containing 15 acres and upwards has increased enormously since 1841. In fact there are now nearly twice as many small farmers—using the term in what in England would be thought its most modest acceptation—as there were before the famine. This will, undoubtedly, be considered an extraordinary statement, but it is, nevertheless, the fact, that holdings of between 15 and 30 acres have increased by 61,000, or 78 per cent., from 1841 to 1861, and holdings above 30 acres by 109,000, or 224 per cent., during the same period, while those between 5 and 15 acres have decreased by less than half those amounts; the emigration, so far as it has extended to the occupying class at all, having been chiefly confined to the poor people who attempted to get a living out of bits of land ranging from half-an-acre to five or six acres, and whose destiny, no custom, or law of tenant-right, however liberal, could have materially affected.* No doubt, the diminution of the holdings in this last category has been enormous, but even among these, as compared with the area of land under tillage in Ireland, the reduction has not been so startling as it might have first appeared: the proportion amounting, in the case of tenements under five acres, to one per annum on every area of 400 acres; and in the case of holdings under 10 acres to one per annum on every area of 1,600 acres.† Of course, the process has neither

---

* This is sufficiently established by the fact of something like 100,000 holdings of this description having disappeared in Ulster alone.

† It is curious to contrast the view Mr. Mill seems to take of the extinction of very small tenancies, with the language of those who hold up the landlords of Ireland to obloquy for having promoted, within very moderate limits, and as a

been so gradual nor so uniform as this calculation would imply, the principal rush having taken place immediately after the potato failure, and from those districts most exposed to its effects; the devastation among the small tenements of Ulster being as tremendous as in any other part of Ireland. Allowing, however, for all subsidiary corrections, it is very evident that so far from the landlords being responsible for the entire emigration, they held no relation, good or bad, with perhaps three-fourths of those who went, even though you counted as emigrants every man, woman, and child that may have quitted—whether of their own free will or on compulsion—the agricultural tenancies that have been extinguished.

But it is well known that vast numbers of the cottier tenantry, instead of emigrating, were converted into labourers, and either found employment in the neighbourhood of their birthplace or removed into adjoining towns, or came over to England, while hundreds of others were placed in possession of some of the 160,000 farms which, as already stated, have been reconstructed since the famine year; thereby reducing still further the number of the land-occupying class who have taken part in emigration, and who probably with their families have never amounted to one-fourth of the entire number.

This moderate share taken by the tenantry in the emigration from Ireland has decreased during the last ten or twelve years, and it is probable that for the last twelve or thirteen years no more than three or four per cent. of the total number of emigrants have been holders of land.

Such a conclusion is, of course, quite contrary to the popular belief, but it is, nevertheless, a fact within the cognizance of every one who is acquainted with the subject. Judge Longfield states it over and over again. He is asked if he knows that a great deal of emigration from Ireland has been going on. " Yes," he replies, " but I do not think that the emigration is much caused by the landlord and tenant question." Again he is asked if good tenants have not been driven away from the country by the supposed

general rule, by the most legitimate and humane means the very improvement he desiderates.

"The principal change in the situation consists in the great diminution, *holding out a hope of the entire extinction*, of cottier tenure. The enormous decrease in the number of small holdings, and increase in those of a medium size, attested by the statistical returns, sufficiently proves the general fact, and all testimonies show that the tendency still continues."—*Mill's Polit. Economy, p.* 413, Vol. i.

insecurity of the tenure. He answers, " In some instances an active man *may* have been prevented from investing his capital in Ireland on that account, but I do not think that class form a large proportion of the emigrants as yet," and a little further on he calculates the emigrants who belong to the tenant-farmer class as amounting to about four out of every 100 persons who quit Ireland, the great bulk of the exodus being composed of small tradesmen, artisans, and labourers.

Happily, the case admits of even closer proof. In the denunciatory addresses with which all are so familiar, the tenant of Ulster is justly indicated as occupying an exceptionally good position, and many have declared they would be satisfied if the tenantry of the south could obtain, under an Act of Parliament, one-tenth of the security accorded by custom to the tenantry of Ulster. If, therefore, the oppression and legalized injustice which is supposed to desolate the homesteads of the south, is absent from the north, it would be natural to imagine that the extinction of tenancies in Ulster would have been *infinitesimal ;* but as a matter of fact the havoc amongst the small farmers of Ulster during the first few years succeeding the potato failure was as portentous as in any other province in Ireland, for whereas in Leinster only 44,514, in Munster 85,929, in Connaught 78,958 holdings between one and fifteen acres disappeared, in Ulster as many as 95,429 have been obliterated. If we restrict the comparison to holdings between one and *five* acres, Ulster's sinister pre-eminence over Leinster and Munster is still maintained, nearly twice as many holdings of this description having been extinguished in Ulster as in Munster, and almost three times as many as in Leinster, the numbers being in Leinster 27,007, in Munster 44,956, in Ulster 74,650, and Connaught 81,786.

It has been urged that the foregoing figures prove nothing, inasmuch as Ulster contains a farming population largely in excess of that of Munster and Connaught, and nearly twice as numerous as that of Leinster, and that we must ignore the fact of nearly 100,000 small holdings having disappeared in Ulster, on the ground that they formed a smaller per-centage on the total number of farms in that Province than did those which have succumbed to a similar fate in Munster, Leinster, and Connaught, to the total number of farms in their respective Provinces.

If this latter statement were correct, it would not be a valid objection. Every one is aware that the agriculture of the North has always been in a sounder state than that of the South and West. But as it happens even the *proportionate* obliteration between 1841 and 1868 of the very small holdings in Ulster, viz., of those between one and five acres, has been 19 per cent. greater than what it was in Leinster, within 3·5 per cent. of what it was in Munster, only 7·7 per cent. below what it was in Connaught, and almost identical with the general average for the kingdom. It is true, if we ascend to the next class of farms, viz., those between 5 and 15 acres, or if we take the farms of all sizes which have been extinguished in the four provinces between the same years, Ulster—as might have been expected—will show a more favourable per-centage, the proportionate decrease being 16·5 per cent. in Ulster, against 16·6 per cent. in Leinster, 30·4 per cent. in Munster, and 22·7 per cent. in Connaught; but when it is remembered that the absolute number of extinguished farms represented by these per-centages is 38·992 in Ulster, as compared with 22,374 in Leinster, 35·388 in Connaught, and 49·816 in Munster, it will be admitted that even from this point of view the share borne by the prosperous tenantry of Ulster in the general calamity sufficiently shows with what impartial severity every part of Ireland was visited, and how unfair it is to attribute solely to the oppression of the landlords of the South a disaster which wrought an enormous, though perhaps not an equal, amount of ruin, in those districts where their malign influence is acknowledged not to prevail.*

But the measure of the Irish landlord's responsibility is not allowed to be limited by the decrease of agricultural holdings; nay, though it appears from the census returns that during a period of ten successive years, ending in 1861, the number of farms in Ireland actually increased, we are still told that because a considerable portion of the population is leaving the country, its departure cannot possibly be occasioned by any other cause than the consolidating policy of the landlords. Let us then continue the application of the test made use of in the preceding paragraph. If emigration is only occasioned by landlord oppression, Ulster ought to have enjoyed a comparative immunity from the general depletion. But what is the fact? Although immediately after

		Holdings in 1841.	Holdings in 1868.	Decrease	Decrease per cent.
* Leinster,	.	134,780	112,406	22,374	16·6
Munster,	.	163,886	114,070	49,816	30·4
Ulster,	.	236,697	197,702	38,992	16·5
Connaught,	.	155,842	120,454	38,388	22·7

the famine the emigration from the South was, for obvious reasons, in excess—though not very largely—of that from the North, the first wave of emigration that ever left the shores of Ireland proceeded from the Protestants of Ulster,* and during the last eighteen years Ulster's contribution to the general emigration has been greater than that of either Connaught or Leinster, and in the ratio of about seven to six as compared with the average of the three other provinces.

But the greater density of the population of Ulster may be again suggested in mitigation of this comparison. Such a consideration hardly alters the result. The ratio of emigration from Ulster to the population of that province has been greater than the ratio of emigration to population from Leinster and Connaught, though less than that from Munster in the proportion nearly of 1 to 2.†

Parliament and unjust landlords, we are told, are depopulating the South: what occult agencies are effecting a similar operation in the North?

There is yet another method at our disposal of testing the justice of these accusations.

By a recent Statute, it has been enacted that no eviction shall take place in Ireland without the intervention of the Sheriff, who is bound to register every operation of the kind. This improvement in the law did not occur until March, 1865. Consequently, although we have Sheriffs' lists of evictions for some years back, they are more or less imperfect until we come to the returns for the year 1865, which have been kept in accordance with the Act of Parliament in all the counties of Ireland except four. Of the evictions in these four counties we can arrive at a sufficiently correct estimate by an independent process.

* See Arthur Young's "Tour in Ireland," and Sir G. C. Lewis on Irish disturbances.

Per cent.

† Ratio of Emigrants from Leinster 1851 to 1868

$$\frac{352,160}{1,412,923} = 24 \cdot 9$$

To Population of Leinster in 1868

Ratio of Emigrants from Connaught 1851 to 1868

$$\frac{228,775}{903,679} = 24 \cdot 4$$

To Population of Connaught in 1868

Ratio of Emigrants from Ulster from 1851 to 1868

$$\frac{495,540}{1,905,815} = 26 \cdot$$

To Population of Ulster in 1868

Ratio of Emigrants from Munster 1851 to 1868

$$\frac{706,054}{1,358,124} = 51 \cdot 9$$

To Population of Munster in 1868

TABLE showing the Sheriffs' Return of Evictions actually executed in the year 1865.

	Actual return of Evictions executed by Sheriffs		Actual return of Evictions executed by Sheriffs	
	In Counties	In Counties of Cities and Counties of Towns	In Counties	In Counties of Cities and Counties of Towns
Carlow	11	...		
Dublin	15	...		
Dublin, City of	...	42		
Kildare	20	...		
Kilkenny	56	...		
Kilkenny, City of	...	3		
King's County	25	...		
Longford	55	...		
Louth	*23	...		
Drogheda, Co. of the Town of	...	5		
Meath	27	...		
Queen's County	30	...		
Westmeath	15	...		
Wexford	54	...		
Wicklow	14	...		
LEINSTER			345	50
Clare	19	...		
Cork	71	...		
Cork, City of	...	14		
Limerick	*66	...		
Limerick, City of	...	...		
Kerry	25	...		
Tipperary†	36	...		
Waterford	22	...		
Waterford, City of	...	5		
MUNSTER			239	19
Antrim	11	...		
Armagh	92	...		
Cavan	36	...		
Donegal	100	...		
Down	29	...		
Fermanagh	25	...		
Londonderry	36	...		
Monaghan	25	...		
Tyrone	*130	...		
ULSTER			484	...
Galway	48	...		
Leitrim	47	...		
Mayo	72	...		
Roscommon	*79	...		
Sligo	20	...		
CONNAUGHT			266	...
IRELAND			1334	69

* In these instances the Sheriff's returns were imperfect, and the figures have been supplied by assuming that the number of evictions executed equalled the entire notices served on the Relieving Officers.

† This is given in the returns as the "County of Clonmel," and it is presumed that Tipperary was meant.

By a previous Act of Parliament every landlord, before proceeding to evict a tenant, was compelled to give notice of his
intentions to the relieving officer of the Union, who kept a return
of all such notifications: these returns extend over the last seven
years, and have been presented to Parliament. Of course they do
not give us the exact number of actual evictions, because it
frequently happens, when the landlord has resorted to this procedure for the recovery of his rent, that the tenant pays up at the
last moment, and no eviction takes place, though the notice to the
Relieving Officer remains uncancelled. During the first three
years of the series great neglect occurred in making up the lists,
and even for the last year no information is supplied from a
considerable number of the electoral divisions. Luckily, however,
the returns of the relieving officers from the four counties, for
which the Sheriffs made no returns, happen to be perfect, and more
than supply the links necessary to complete the list of evictions
for the whole of Ireland during the past year, as will be seen on
reference to the opposite table. With the exception of those for
Dublin, and a few other places, no distinction has been made
between the urban and the agricultural evictions, though for the
purposes of the present argument such an analysis would have
been desirable. On the other hand the return of evictions during
a single year is not altogether a safe guide to an average over a
longer period. Let us then convert the figures with which we
are furnished for 1865, into a round number, and take the general
rate of rural evictions in Ireland at about 1,500 per annum, which
is probably considerably in excess of the truth.—(See Table.)

The total emigration from Ireland has averaged during the same
interval about 90,000 a year. If therefore this emigration has
been so swollen by evictions, the annual average of such evictions
ought to be proportionate to that emigration; but the average of
evictions during the same period, as compared with the number of
emigrants, has been at the rate of about two to every 100. That
is to say, among every 100 persons who have left Ireland during
the last six years about ten persons, if we include the family of
each individual dealt with, have done so under the compulsion of a
landlord. In other words, and to display the case still more
explicitly in relation to the whole subject, during the only period
for which we have trustworthy statistics, evictions have been
effected (supposing the responsibility for them be distributed over
the entire landlord class, which is the theory insisted on) at the

rate of one, once in every five years, on each estate; or, to put the case geographically, at the rate of one a year over every area of 10,000 acres of occupied land. It is further to be remarked that evictions have been fewest in Munster, the Province from whence the largest emigration has taken place.*

Not only, however, do we know the number of evictions during the last ten years, but we also know what proportion of these evictions was necessitated by the non-payment of rent. It is true the returns which give this information again confound the urban with the rural districts, but it may fairly be supposed that the same proportions prevailed in either category; and if that be taken for granted, it would appear that of the total number of evictions which the landlords have effected in Ireland two-thirds were for non-payment of rent.

When, therefore, it is considered how many are the other contingencies,—such as the infraction of covenants, intolerably bad cultivation, subletting and illegal squatting, which not only entitle but render it incumbent on a landlord, from time to time, to free his estates of an undesirable tenant; and the extraordinary number of tenants on each estate, which of course must multiply the chances of collision, it is impossible not to come to the conclusion that the annual rate of evictions for other cause than that of non-payment of rent, whether taken with reference to the number of occupiers, or to the extent of the area occupied,—in the one case amounting to about 0·1 per cent. per annum, in the other to about one eviction per annum to 30,000 acres, proves conclusively that the relations of the landlords of Ireland with their

* Returns have been received from the Clerks of the Peace of the several counties in Ireland of the number of civil bill ejectment decrees on notices to qnit obtained at the several Quarter Sessions in the years 1866, 1867, 1868, and 1869, from which it appears that the average annual number in all Ireland during these years has been, as nearly as possible, 1 in every 880 agricultural tenements ; and from the returns of the sub-sheriffs it appears that only about 1 in every 2,000—being less than one-half of the decrees so obtained—have been executed. One remarkable feature, however, in those returns is, that while in Ulster the proportion of ejectment decrees against agricultural tenements is so high as 1 in 610, in Leinster, Munster, and Connaught the proportion is only 1 in 1,220, the relative proportion of those executed being about the same in each of the four Provinces. Out of every 10 decrees executed, 7 were for non-payment of rent, and 3 on notices to quit, the average amount of rent due when the process issued being about 2½ years. These returns do not support the allegation that agrarian disturbances are generally traceable to evictions or clearances by landlords, the fact being that where evictions are more rare agrarian disturbances are more frequent; and in Ulster, the Province proverbially most free from such disturbances, evictions have been twice as numerous as in any of the others. It is evident, therefore, that these outrages must have some other origin than " the eviction of the rural population by their landlords."

tenantry are by no means on that uncomfortable footing which is alleged, and that to describe Ireland as "*a land of evictions*" is to adopt an expression calculated to convey a false impression.

But it is now objected that though the list of evictions may not witness so conclusively as might be desired to the tale of oppression, that a record of evictions is, after all, but an incomplete indication of what is going on, and that it is the fear of eviction which uproots the people, before the landlords have occasion to put in motion the machinery of the law. The difficulty of disproving so indefinite a charge is obvious. The fact that more than a decade has passed without diminishing by a single tenancy the number of farms in Ireland, is not likely to make much impression on those who have started this new theory. Still less would the inference that no landlord can have an interest in dispossessing a good tenant who pays his rent do so. Fortunately for the cause of truth, we have positive evidence on this point. It is the practice of the Custom House authorities in their register of the persons embarking for foreign countries carefully to note their previous occupations. Now, it appears from these returns, which extend as far back as the year 1854, that the total number of the farming class who have quitted the United Kingdom during the 13 years preceding 1867, amounted to 86,388 persons, that is to say, to about 4 per cent. of the total emigration. Even supposing, therefore, that no English or Scotch farmer were included in the category, the total number of occupiers leaving the ports of Britain would only form *eight* per cent. of the emigration from Ireland alone; but the analysis by the Emigration Commissioners of the nationality of the agriculturists who emigrated during the years 1865 and 1866, shows that the Irish element was very little in excess of the British, and that the total number of Irish occupiers who sailed from any part of the United Kingdom was exactly $2\frac{1}{2}$ per cent. of the Irish emigration during the same period.

In fact, turn the matter as you will—apply what test you please —start from whatever point you choose—all the evidence converges to the same conclusion, and establishes beyond a doubt that out of every 100 persons who cross the Atlantic (a very large proportion of whom consist of gentlemen, professional men, merchants, &c.), not more than two or three are induced to do so by any difficulties which may have arisen out of their relations with their landlords.*

---

* Total number of Farmers who have emigrated from the United Kingdom in 1864 7,245
    Total number whom the Commissioners have classed as Gentlemen, Professional Men, Merchants, &c. 5,842

CHAPTER III.

ECONOMIC HISTORY OF IRELAND.

WE have shown that the "exterminating policy" of the Irish landlords has resulted in the existence, at the census of 1861, of a greater number of holdings of all sizes in Ireland than there were in 1851, and of 160,000 more tenant farmers of fifteen acres and upwards than there were twenty years ago, the smallest area which, in the unanimous opinion of Judge Longfield, of Mr. Dillon, of Mr. M'Carthy Downing, of the Catholic Bishop of Cloyne, and of Mr. Curling, can be cultivated with advantage, or over which those gentlemen would themselves be willing to extend the protection of a lease. But it is said by some that the real accusations against the landlord class in Ireland, so ruthlessly gibbeted, is not exactly for their own acts, but as representatives of those bygone generations to whose vicious mismanagement of their estates the present misfortunes of the country are to be attributed. That such is not the issue raised in the various manifestoes alluded to will be at once apparent on referring to them; but, as it may be useful to ascertain what have been some of the historical sources of Ireland's *economic* difficulties, let us endeavour to discriminate between the share in them attributable to the former owners of the soil and that which is due to other causes.

The writer who thus proposes to antedate our responsibilities seems satisfied he has arrived at the fountain-head of Ireland's calamities when he points his finger at the Irish proprietary of former days; nor does he dream of inquiring whether the landlord of 70 or 80 years ago may not himself have been a creature of circumstances, involved in the complexities of a system of which he was as much the victim as his tenants. The popular conception of the Irish country gentleman of former days is principally derived from works of fiction and caricature, and is probably as correct as is usual with information gathered from such sources. In many respects it stands in favourable juxtaposition with the picture drawn of his English contemporary by Macaulay, though the noxious influences which emanated from the policy pursued by England towards the Catholics of Ireland must have been as demoralizing to him as it was to every other member of the dominant community. But it is alleged that the practical results of his dealing with his property have been over-population, rack-rents, and an exodus of 2,000,000 souls. The question is, have these phenomena followed in such direct sequence as is alleged, or have other influences, independent of the landlord's agency, vitiated a system which otherwise would not have been unhealthy? Now, of the three evils he is supposed to have occasioned, the two last are the direct consequences of the first. A rack-rent is the product of competition, and both competition and emigration are the results of over-population. The true measure, therefore, of the responsibility of the Irish landlord is the share he has had in disturbing the equilibrium which ought to have been maintained between the increase of population and the development of the country's industrial resources.

As a matter of fact, it does not appear that the Irish landlords of former days dealt harshly with their tenantry. Even Mr. Butt admits that during the whole of the 18th century there were scarcely any evictions, and that long leases were almost universal; while Judge Longfield states that so late as 1835 there was very little land in the southern and western counties not on lease, and that "*most of the leases were all in the tenants' favour.*" Nor is it alleged that the landlords themselves exacted exorbitant rents; the principal complaint against them is that they leased their lands to middlemen, and that sometimes they were separated from the actual occupiers of the soil by a dozen derivative tenures. From this fact it is evident that the rents they charged must have been comparatively moderate. But long leases at moderate rates are hardly a criminal arrangement. It is true the increasing pressure of a teeming population, and the natural instinct which, Judge Longfield tells us, is inherent in every Irish tenant—to turn himself into a landlord if he gets the chance—resulted in a state of things replete with mischief. But for the development of this unexpected phase in the Irish land system, the proprietor is by no means responsible to the degree which is supposed. Up to nearly the close of the last century the great proportion of the country was in pasture, and the population was less than half of what it amounted to in 1841. The holdings were of considerable size, and when a farm was let the landlord never dreamt of its being converted into tillage, and no provisions against subdivision were introduced. But as population multiplied the situation changed, and the enormous rise in the price of grain and provisions on the breaking out of the French war made it the interest of the tenant

to subdivide his land as minutely as he could. He accordingly
introduced an Irish edition of what is known as " la petite culture."
It is true most of the latter leases contained clauses against subletting, but an unexpected legal subtlety rendered them practically
inoperative, and when attempts were made to stop an innovation,
which in no way benefited the landlord, most proprietors found,
after going to great expense, that they were completely powerless.
The practice consequently spread, and an obnoxious class of middlemen, as they were termed, re-let the greater proportion of the soil
of Ireland at rack-rents to their teeming countrymen, in small
holdings sometimes less than half an acre. But though the
majority of middlemen became constituted in this manner, there is
no doubt that sometimes they were placed in possession of land by
the owners, with the express intention that they should sublet, and
it is with this method of procedure adopted by a few that the
entire class have been credited. Though, however, the experiment
turned out unsuccessfully, there was nothing at the time to warn
the proprietor against it, and it can be easily conceived that many
a landlord, speaking neither the same language, nor professing the
religion as his tenants, might consider it not only a very convenient
but a very popular alternative to give a long lease at a low rent to
some person less alien to the peasants in race and religion than
himself, upon the understanding that he might relet it in smaller
areas. If the event proved unfortunate, it was not because the
tenant was a middleman, but because he dealt with his comrades
and co-religionists more unmercifully than might have been
expected.*

Whether even the middleman is deserving of all the abuse
which is heaped upon him may be a question. To drive a hard
bargain is a failing not confined to that class of persons; and,
perhaps, the moral responsibility of accepting a competition rent is
pretty much the same as that of profiting by the market rate of
wages. If the first is frequently exorbitant, the latter is often
inadequate, and inadequate wages are as fatal to efficiency as a rack
rent is to production; though each be the result of voluntary
adjustment, it is the same abject misery and absence of an alternative which rule the rate of both; if the unhappy condition of the

---

* Besides the subletting by middlemen for a profit (the case with which we are now
dealing), subletting, or subdivision, took place extensively by parents as a provision
for their children on marriage. Holdings of even one acre were sometimes thus subdivided. The reports of the Devon Commission teem with evidence to this effect.

Irish cottier tenant of former days may be referred to the one, the
physical and mental degradation of the labouring classes in the
Black Country, as revealed in the report of a late Commission, is
even a more startling illustration of the other.

In fact the middlemen of Ireland were rather the exponents than
the cause of the people's misery, and, though piled ten deep one
above the other, on a single tenancy, they no more occasioned rack-
rents than the degrees on a barometer occasion the atmospheric
pressure they record. Derivative tenancies, cottier allotments,
potato cultivation, low wages, emigration, have been the rude
alleviations—not the origin—of the country's destitution; just as
half-rations are the alternative for short provisions—or any wages
are preferable to starvation—a patch of ground, at a rack-rent, to
serfdom and 3d. a day—and a free farm in America to digging
another man's potato garden in Connemara. Similar phenomena
would have declared themselves under any system of land tenure,
and in any country where the population had expanded in a degree
disproportionate to its capacities for self-sustentation. If it were
otherwise, every perpetuity in Ireland would be a land of Goshen,*
and Ulster a paradise where rack-rents and evictions were unknown.
But it is an acknowledged fact, proved by evidence of proprietors
and farmers, that the low-let perpetuities of the South and West
only exaggerate the worst features of the worst estates, and in
Ulster, though under a more subtle guise, rack-rents and the
middleman are as rampant as they used to be in Connaught.

This last statement requires explanation. In Ulster it is the
custom for the incoming tenant to pay the outgoing tenant a sum
of money—nominally, for his improvements, really—for an inde-
terminate value called his "goodwill." If the worth of the
improvement corresponded with the amount of the payment, the
arrangement would be unobjectionable. But it seldom does. An
incoming tenant will give openly, or surreptitiously, £5, £10, or
£20 an acre for land let at a high rent, in a bad condition, and
without improvements, the figure generally increasing in an inverse
ratio to the size of the farm and the poverty of the district, the
largest tenant prices prevailing in Donegal, and the most moderate

* "It does not appear either, as a general rule, from the evidence, that those
tenants who have the longest leases, and the most beneficial interest in their farms,
have brought the lands they hold to a more productive or improved state than others,
not possessing such advantages or security. It is even broadly asserted by many that
lands held under long leases, at a nominal rent, are in a worse state than those held
from year to year."— *Digest Devon Commission, Summary,* p. 16.

in Down, while the payment is almost invariably made with money borrowed at a high rate of interest. This interest is, of course, a second or rack-rent paid to the lender of the purchase money (who is frequently given the use of a portion of the land as a security for his interest and the repayment of the loan), and the recipient who walks off with it is neither more nor less than a bastard middleman, who takes a fine in lieu of an annual payment for a non-existing value. As a consequence, the new tenant commences his enterprise burdened with debt and destitute of capital, and with a mortgagee in possession of part of the land. Hence low farming, inadequate profits, uneducated children, and, too frequently, the ruin and emigration of the Ulster tenant, in spite of indulgent landlords and a secure tenure.

It is amusing to observe that the same persons who are anxious to mitigate the effects of competition by imposing on the owner of the land a rent fixed by Act of Parliament, always contend that the person in whose favour this beneficial interest is to be created should have the right to dispose of it to the highest bidder: that is to say, though I am to be precluded from receiving the market value of my land,—my tenant is to be allowed to do so, by extracting a fine from whoever may be induced to make the most extravagant offer for his good-will. It is hardly perhaps to be expected that the advocates of such measures should condescend to show how far their proposals are compatible with justice, and the narrowest interpretations of the rights of property, but at least they ought to prove them conducive to the agricultural prosperity of the country, and consonant with public policy. But as the result of such an arrangement would be to fill the majority of the farms in Ireland, in the course of a few years, with tenants paying a double rent, *i.e.*, the Parliamentary rent to their landlords, and the interest on the fine squeezed out of them by the lucky individual to whom Parliament had attributed a share in the original owner's proprietary rights, it is difficult to see what could be the advantage of the change. It may indeed be urged that the vice in the system would only blaze into life on a change of tenancy:—but changes of tenancy are continually taking place:— not only by the surrender of farms, but on the death of every occupant. His sons succeed:—they all consider they have an equal claim to the holding:—if permitted they subdivide it;—if not the eldest has to pay the others their share of the father's beneficial interest; and the competition price is their standard of valuation. Consequently the permanent tenant finds himself in the same position as if he had bought the farm from a stranger:—that is to say, destitute of capital and probably in debt:—while the brothers walk off with a sum of money which, if the rent is as fair as the theory of the arrangement pre-supposes, can represent no real value, and to which therefore they have much less right than the landlord, whom it has been the intention of Parliament to debar from such exactions. Now, it is not pretended that the imposition of rack-rents is at all a general practice with proprietors. The high value of the goodwill on many estates is the index of the landlord's moderation, and his virtues are put up to auction in the same lot with his land. The rents of Ireland are comparatively low, and fines, which is the worst form of rent, are rarely, if ever, taken: to transfer therefore the power of exaction created by competition from the landlord, against whose interest it is to enforce it, and to hand it over to the tenant, who would never fail to do so, would hardly be a change for the better; yet so little is this question understood that you will hear the same person who would vehemently denounce a landlord for insisting on a rack-rent, detail with complacency the enormous sums of money which this or that person has obtained for his tenant-right, from some ill-advised successor to his farm, whom he has skinned by the process, and left stranded for life on the barren acres.* Yet it is in the prosperity of this latter individual—on whose solvency the proper cultivation of the land will depend, rather than in that of the outgoing tenant—that both the landlord and the community is interested.

From the foregoing considerations it is apparent that competition is an irrepressible force:† that if stifled in one direction, it will

* "It is, in the great majority of cases, not a reimbursement for outlay incurred, or improvements effected on the land, but a mere life insurance or purchase of immunity from outrage. Hence, the practice is more accurately and significantly termed, ' selling the good-will.'

"And *it is not uncommon for a tenant without a lease to sell the bare privilege of occupancy or possession of his farm without any visible sign of improvement having been made by him, at from ten to sixteen, up to twenty and even forty years' purchase of the rent."—Dig. Dev. Com.*

† The following conclusions are given in the Summary of the Evidence before the Devon Commission:—

"That small holdings, in consequence of the greater competition, command a higher price than large.

"That the tenant-right confuses the rights of landlord and tenant, and is an undue interference with the interest of the proprietor.

burst out in another; that a system of compulsory rents would only lead to its manifestation, in a more objectionable form; and that, as a matter of policy, it is better that those alone should have the opportunity of taking advantage of it, who are the least likely to abuse their power.

Wherever you go the same deleterious influence signalizes its presence by analogous, if not by identical effects. In the South and West the poison has infiltrated the system itself, breeding monstrous excrescences in the shape of the middleman and the rack-rented cottier. In the North it has manifested its presence by a parasitical growth of inflated tenant-right prices, as effectually fatal to the healthy expansion of our agricultural industry. The original cause of the disease is everywhere the same. The disproportion of the opportunities of employment to population has resulted in universal pressure and universal competition—competition in the labour market, already modified by emigration; competition in the land market—only to be relieved by the application to more profitable occupations of so much of the productive energies of the nation as may be in excess of the requirements of a perfect agriculture.

But, it may be objected that even though emigration, rack-rents —and their natural result—low farming, are equally rife under every description of tenure, and cannot therefore wholly be set down to the pernicious influence of the owners of landed property, yet, some human agency must be accountable for the perennial

"That the amount paid for the purchase of tenant-right injures the incoming tenant, by diminishing his capital.

"That debts are contracted upon the security of the tenant-right.

"That the children of farmers are provided for by charges upon the tenant-right.

"That the incoming tenant is frequently compelled to borrow funds for the purchase of the tenant-right at usurious interest.

"That the existence of the tenant-right renders more difficult reclamation of waste lands by capitalists.

"That in most parts of Ireland the practice exists of selling the possession of farms held even from year to year.

"That the price of tenant-right frequently amounts to £10, £12, £20, or £25 per acre, and that sometimes as much as forty years' purchase of the rent is paid for it.

"That many proprietors have attempted to regulate and restrict its price.

"That such restrictions are frequently evaded.

"That the tenant is able to obtain a high rate of purchase for his good-will where he has effected no improvements, or has even deteriorated his farm.

"That even if the price of tenant-right be at all affected by the improvements made on a farm (a fact doubted by some witnesses), it is not so influenced in proportion to the value of the improvements."—*Dig. Devon Com.* p. 290.

desolation of a lovely and fertile island, watered by the fairest streams, caressed by a clement atmosphere, held in the embraces of a sea whose affluence fills the noblest harbours of the world, and inhabited by a race—valiant, generous, tender—gifted beyond measure with the power of physical endurance, and graced with the liveliest intelligence.

The discovery of this enigma and its solution may possibly give answer to the famous question originally put to the Kilkenny Parliament, and lately repeated with considerable point by Mr. Bright—" How is it that the King is none the richer for Ireland?"

Of course, any perfect retrospect of the economic career of Ireland would necessarily involve a review of her political and religious history, but so large a treatment of the subject would not be adapted to the present cursory discussion. Let us briefly point out what those influences have been which have as effectually stunted the development of our material prosperity as penal laws and religious intolerance have vitiated our social atmosphere—the commercial jealousies of Great Britain.

It has been rather the custom of late to represent the landed interests of Great Britain as the sole inventors and patentees of protection. The experience of Ireland does not confirm this theory. During the course of the last 250 years we have successively tasted the tender mercies of every interest in turn— whether landed, trading, or commercial—and have little reason to pronounce one less selfish than another. From Queen Elizabeth's reign until within a few years of the Union the various commercial confraternities of Great Britain never for a moment relaxed their relentless grip on the trades of Ireland. One by one, each of our nascent industries was either strangled in its birth, or handed over, gagged and bound, to the jealous custody of the rival interest in England, until at last every fountain of wealth was hermetically sealed, and even the traditions of commercial enterprise have perished through desuetude.

The owners of England's pastures opened the campaign. As early as the commencement of the 16th century the beeves of Roscommon, Tipperary, and Queen's County undersold the produce of the English grass counties in their own market. By an Act of the 20th of Elizabeth Irish cattle were declared a " nuisance," and their importation was prohibited. Forbidden to send our beasts alive across the Channel, we killed them at home, and began to supply the sister country with cured provisions. A second Act of

Parliament imposed prohibitory duties on salted meats. The hides of the animals still remained, but the same influence soon put a stop to the importation of leather. Our cattle trade abolished, we tried sheep farming. The sheep breeders of England immediately took alarm, and Irish wool was declared contraband by a Parliament of Charles II. Headed in this direction we tried to work up the raw material at home, but this created the greatest outcry of all. Every maker of fustian, flannel, and broadcloth in the country rose up in arms, and by an Act of William III. the woollen industry of Ireland was extinguished, and 20,000 manufacturers left the island. The easiness of the Irish labour market and the cheapness of provisions still giving us an advantage, even though we had to import our materials, we next made a dash at the silk business; but the silk manufacturer proved as pitiless as the woolstaplers. The cotton manufacturer, the sugar refiner, the soap and candle maker (who especially dreaded the abundance of our kelp), and any other trade or interest that thought it worth its while to petition was received by Parliament with the same partial cordiality, until the most searching scrutiny failed to detect a single vent through which it was possible for the hated industry of Ireland to respire. But, although excluded from the markets of Britain, a hundred harbours gave her access to the universal sea. Alas! a rival commerce on her own element was still less welcome to England, and as early as the reign of Charles II. the Levant, the ports of Europe, and the oceans beyond the Cape were forbidden to the flag of Ireland. The colonial trade alone was in any manner open—if that could be called an open trade which for a long time precluded all exports whatever, and excluded from direct importation to Ireland such important articles as sugar, cotton, and tobacco. What has been the consequence of such a system, pursued with relentless pertinacity for 250 years, whereby, in the words of Mr. Cobden, "England, by discouraging the commerce of Ireland—thus striking at the very root of civilization —made herself responsible for much of the barbarisms that afflicts it?" This: that, debarred from every other trade and industry, the entire nation flung itself back upon "*the land*" with as fatal an impulse as when a river whose current is suddenly impeded rolls back and drowns the valley it once fertilized.

For a long time, however, the limits of their own island proved sufficient for the three or four millions which then inhabited it. The cheapness of provisions in Ireland used to be the bugbear of the English manufacturer. But each successive century found the nation more straitened within its borders. At last a choice had to be made between the sacrifice of domestic happiness or of physical comfort; the natural liveliness of their affections, combined with a buoyant temperament, led the people to accept the latter alternative. The mildness of the climate, the cheapness of the fuel, and above all, the suitableness of the potato to what is technically called " la petite culture," contributed to turn the scale, and early marriages continued to remain a characteristic of the Irish peasantry. Even had the landlords interfered, their remonstrances would have been in vain, and, the downward impulse once communicated, acquired a continually accelerated momentum, for the simple reason that each succeeding generation was accustomed from infancy to a lower standard of comfort than that which had satisfied their fathers. Extraneous circumstances, such as the rise of prices during the French wars, stimulated the popular tendency to self expansion, until, by a logical sequence of events, the spectacle was presented of a nation doubling its population every fifty years, yet entirely dependent for its support upon an agricultural area which had been found barely sufficient for its needs when it was a third less numerous; under such conditions, high rents, low wages, and all the other indications of destitution would be as inevitable as famine prices in a beleaguered city.

But we may be told this frantic clinging of the Irish to the land is natural to their genius, and not a result of commercial restrictions. History supplies the perfect refutation of such a theory: Though the hostile tariff of England comprehended almost every article produced in Ireland, one single exception was permitted. From the reign of William III. the linen trade of Ireland has been free; as a consequence, at this day Irish linens are exported in enormous quantities to every quarter of the globe, and their annual value nearly equals half the rental of the island.

Many attempts were made by the rival interest in England to deprive us of this boon, and in 1785 a petition—signed by 117,000 persons—was presented by Manchester, praying for the prohibition of Irish linens, but justice and reason for once prevailed, and the one surviving industry of Ireland was spared. How has it repaid the clemency of the British Parliament? By dowering the crown of England with as fair a cluster of flourishing towns and loyal centres of industry as are to be found in any portion of the Empire. Would you see what Ireland might have been—go to Derry, to

Belfast, to Lisburn, and by the exceptional prosperity which has been developed, not only within a hundred towns and villages, but for miles and miles around them, you may measure the extent of the injury we have sustained. Would you ascertain how the numerical strength of a nation may be multiplied, while the status of each individual that comprises it is improved,—go to Belfast, where (within a single generation) the population has quadrupled, and the wages of labour have more than doubled.

How powerfully the development of manufactures in the North of Ireland has contributed to the relief of the agricultural classes of Ulster, by giving the tenant-farmer an opportunity of apprenticing some of his sons to business instead of sub-dividing among them his diminutive holding, by enabling the cottier tenant to supplement his agricultural earnings with hand-loom weaving, and by a general alleviation of the pressure upon the land, need not be described. These and many other considerations force on us the conviction— that had Ireland only been allowed to develop the other innumerable resources at her command, as she has developed the single industry in which she was permitted to embark, the equilibrium between the land and the population dependent upon the land would never have been disturbed, nor would the relations between landlord and tenant have become a subject of anxiety.

In dealing with the economic interests of a great country, it is on the essential forces which are producing specific results, rather than on the capricious accidents of the situation, that we must fix our attention.

If, on consideration, it should be found that the responsibilities of the landed proprietors for the ills of Ireland have been grossly exaggerated, if the instances of harshness and mismanagement laid to the charge of individual landlords by men of the highest honour, though we may deplore their existence, are so manifestly exceptional as to have produced an inappreciable effect on the current of events we are considering, let us have sufficient faith in the generosity of their accusers to believe that they will rejoice rather than regret to discover that so numerous and important a section of their fellow-countrymen neither are nor have been unworthy of their esteem; the rather that our conclusions on such a point cannot materially affect any pending controversy between the landlords and their tenantry. If an alteration is to be made in the tenure of land in Ireland, that alteration must be founded on abstract principles of justice, and the requirements of present policy. It would be as great an outrage to visit with penal legislation the recent purchaser of a property in the Incumbered Estates' Court because fifty years ago the grandfather of the former proprietor created 40s. freeholders (a tenure of which Mr. Butt speaks almost with approval) and took the best rent, as it would be to load the woollen manufacturers of Lancashire with the responsibility of Ireland's misfortunes because the particular industry in which they are interested owes more than any other its present prosperity to the cruel policy towards Ireland inagurated by their predecessors.

CHAPTER IV.

EVICTION—ARE LANDLORDS OR TENANTS ANSWERABLE ?

WE now come to the third point in our inquiry—viz., whether it is fair to refer the evictions in Ireland to the injustice of the landlords rather than to the neglect of their legitimate obligations on the part of the tenants. What has been already said almost answers this question, while the fact that over two-thirds of the registered ejectments are for non-payment of rent speaks for itself. But as it is the fashion to talk of the act of eviction as if it were a crime, we shall analyse the nature of the operation.

First, let us define the respective rights of landlord and tenant. A landlord is an owner of land which he has either bought himself, or inherited from those who have bought it. In either case, the land he possesses represents a specific amount of capital, accumulated either by his own industry or by that of his forefathers, for which he is content to receive interest at a rate sometimes less than, seldom exceeding, 4 per cent. Considerable prominence has been given of late to the fact that in the time of Elizabeth, Cromwell, and William, extensive confiscations of property took place in Ireland, and it has been more than hinted that such a circumstance might justify the repetition of an analogous process. But, however strongly this argument may appeal to the conscience of the small minority who are able to trace their present proprietorship to an historical source, it will hardly commend itself to those whose possessions represents the mercantile industry of some distant ancestor, improved by centuries of hereditary thrift, or the proceeds of their own exertions invested in land on the faith of a Parliamentary title.

Whether vague suggestions,—which (as far as they mean anything) would imply the uprooting of the whole of the population of Ulster, and the transference of nearly all the landed property of Ireland, from those whose legal title to it is indisputable to a thousand competitors whose claims would rest on distinctions of race and religion, —are calculated to attract capital to the country or promote a feeling of security, it is needless to inquire. Such barren speculations cannot alter the fact that at present the owner of landed property in Ireland holds it in exactly the same sense, and under the same conditions, as the owner of property in England. He can sell his interest in it, he can let it, he can cultivate it himself, as he may please, so long as he does not infringe existing contracts or the laws of his country.

A tenant, on the other hand, is a person who does not possess land, but who hires the use of it. He embarks his capital in another man's field, much in the same way as a trader embarks his merchandise in another man's ship. Experience teaches him that by expending a certain amount of labour and capital in the cultivation of the soil he is able within a limited period to get back from it not only the original capital he had expended, but also a profitable rate of interest upon that capital. What rate that interest may reach will depend on his own skill and discretion, just as the trader's profits will depend on the judgment with which he sorts his cargo or selects his port. In either case, the amount of hire paid for the use of the ship or for the use of the land will be determined by competition, and will affect the balance of gain or loss on both transactions.* If ships are few and land is scarce, freight and rent will rise, and the rise of each will in a great measure be regulated by the disproportion of ships to goods and of farmers to farms. But the rate of freight or the amount of rent are not the only circumstances which will affect the profits of either speculator. In the case of the trader, all will depend on his goods being landed at the port he intended, whilst the most promising expectations of the agriculturist may be ruined unless he retain possession of the land he occupies for a definite period. A clear understanding, therefore, ought to exist in both cases between the parties interested, as to the course of the ship and the duration of

* The illustration in the text must be accepted with the important qualification that the supply of land is fixed and limited, while that of ships can be indefinitely increased. Still, the analogies presented by the two cases are too striking to be omitted.

the tenancy. The shipowner may want to send his vessel to one port and the trader his goods to another, just as the proprietor of an estate may wish to let his land for one term and the tenant to hire it for another. The definitive arrangement will depend upon the respective necessities of the contracting parties and the balance of competition. On the previous supposition that ships are few and land scarce, the advantage of the bargain will remain with the owner of the ship and the possessor of the field—the one consenting to call at the desired port, unforseen contingencies permitting, the other agreeing to let his land on such conditions as may be most suitable to his ulterior views. Both arrangements may be thought by the impartial observer unfavourable to the two interests affected by it—the one to commerce, the other to agriculture—but inasmuch as each was a voluntary contract between persons who must be supposed capable of managing their own affairs, any legislative interference to amend the bargain might occasion greater mischief than it seeks to remedy. For instance, a law requiring the ship to call at certain ports, or the landlord to let his land for what he might consider a longer term than was desirable, would be a grievance to both shipowner and landowner; they would probably protect themselves either by refusing to carry the goods and to let the field, or by raising the rate of the freight and rent. This result would suit neither merchant nor farmer. Parliament might again intervene, and not only lay down the plan of the voyage and the duration of the tenure, but might impose a specified scale of freights and rents, and declare the shipowner incapable of freighting his own ship, and the landlord of tilling his own land. But so violent an interference with the rights of property would be unjust, impracticable, and obviously productive of greater evils than those it was intended to remedy.

If the foregoing illustration be apposite, it follows that the tenant's interest in the farm he hires is like the trader's interest in the ship he charters, is limited in duration. The voyage concluded, the lease expired, both ship and field revert to their respective owners.

It is hardly reasonable to deny the analogy on the ground that the ship is a manufactured article, but the earth is the gift of God. The land I have bought is probably itself as much a manufactured article as the ship: and the iron or wood of which the ship is built is as much the gift of God as the land: the labour or enterprise by which the land has been rendered valuable is as clearly represented by the money I gave for it, as the industry and ingenuity exercised on its construction is represented by the price the owner has paid for the ship. It is true the country of which my estate is part belongs to the nation, and consequently my property in that estate is over-ridden by the imperial rights of the commonwealth. But this fact cannot invest the individual who may happen to hire my land, *when once his tenancy is terminated either by lapse of time or by the violation of his contract*, with any peculiar rights in excess of those which may be inherent in the community at large.

Of course, in the case of land, the desirable duration of a tenant's occupancy may vary with circumstances, from one year to a hundred; it might equally suit him to take, and me to let, a corner of my park for a single crop, or a bit of pasture for a few months' grazing, or a tract of heather under a reclamation lease of sixty years. But if the principle of the arrangement is to be defined it may be stated as an axiom that, unless otherwise provided for by special agreement, a tenant's *equitable* claim to the occupation of his farm extends to such a period as shall enable him, by ordinary diligence and skill, to put back into his pocket the capital he has expended on its improvement, together with a fair amount of interest upon that capital;* for it is evident, first, that were the profits of agricultural enterprise to be artificially hoisted to a rate of interest beyond the amount appropriate to such investments, the consequent stimulus to competition would immediately reduce them to their normal level; and, secondly, that to

* It is sometimes objected that land having been made valuable by the exertions of the former generations of tenants, the additional fertility thus created ought to devolve like an apostolic succession on the actual occupants. But if the persons referred to conducted their business properly, they have been already remunerated by their annual surplus of profit. The increased value permanently acquired by the land through their exertions, was a subsidiary accident which they neither intended, nor could prevent. *It was in expectation of such a result the land was let to them.* In pursuit of their own interests they happened to disengage the latent virtues of the soil, which were the property of the former owner, and which, after they had been developed, the subsequent purchaser of the estate acquired

For a tenant, therefore, to claim a share in the increased value of the land in addition to his fair profits, would be as unreasonable as for the labourer to claim a share in the tenant's profits in addition to his own wages, on the plea that those profits resulted from the increased fertility communicated to the land by his manual toil. The argument is as cogent in the one case as the other. Moreover, as a matter of fact, though the labour of former tenants may frequently have improved the land, the operations of the actual tenant have as often deteriorated it: and virgin soil that was worth a great deal before a spade had touched it, may become completely exhausted by bad cultivation.

endow the present chance occupiers of farms with an indefeasible tenure would be tantamount to the imposition of a disability on the rest of the non-occupying population to hold land. The tenant's claim to occupation being necessarily, then, of a terminable character, he has no right to complain if his landlord finds it advisable, *on the expiration of his term*, to confer on another advantages similar to those he has hitherto enjoyed. Many considerations indispose both parties to change their relationship. Ancient associations, habits of friendly intercourse, the fellowship which unites old customers, may preserve the bond for generations; but when once it becomes the imperative interest of either to cancel it, the endeavour of any third party, such as the State, to force the maintenance of a connexion, which in its very nature is one of voluntary obligation, will tend to precipitate the rupture.

It is admitted by the witnesses on the other side that an industrious tenant is seldom, if ever, turned off an estate in Ireland; but it is a mistake to imagine that non-payment of rent is the only circumstance which can justify evictions. Any one acquainted with the management of land is aware that an idle or unskilful farmer, even though he pay his rent, may do his landlord's property more harm than an industrious tenant, who is occasionally in arrear. Few things are more liable to deterioration than land, and the value of a field may be as completely annihilated—or, in the graphic language of a gentleman before the Land Commission, " the life and soul dragged out of the land "—for a certain number of years, as that of a house off which you take the roof. One of the landlord's most important duties is that of insuring the consummate cultivation of his estate, and to hold him up to obloquy because he makes a point of weeding his property of men whose want of energy, or skill, or capital, renders them incapable of doing their duty by their farms, and replacing them by more suitable tenants is hardly reasonable. Were he not to do so, he might, with more reason, be censured for neglecting his duty to himself and to the State.

Again, the failure of the potatoes, the repeal of the Corn Laws, and the application of steam and machinery to husbandry, have converted a primitive art into a complicated science. If the Irish agriculturist is to hold his own with the foreign producer, it can only be by high farming, a large expenditure of capital, and great economy of labour—conditions of industry almost incompatible with the maintenance of unreasonably small farms. There has consequently arisen a desire on the part of both landlord and occupier to increase existing holdings, and when such a feeling prevails in the minds of the two parties chiefly interested, the tendency will not be arrested by legislation.

" Fifteen years' experience in the management of property in Ireland," observes Lord Dufferin, and the experience of many others will bear him out, " has convinced me that the farmer of 20 acres at a fair rent makes a larger profit, educates his children better, accumulates more capital, and is more contented than the holder of eight or nine acres at the same rent, and that, at least, up to 30 or 40 acres, the advantage continues in an ascending ratio. Many advocates of the small farm system would carry it higher, and almost every tenant on my estate is probably of their opinion. I am by no means disposed to consider the English system of large farms applicable to Ireland ; on the contrary, I believe we shall eventually settle down to an average size of farm, as exceptionally suitable as in the gauge of our railways ; but if a landlord wishes to furnish his estate with farm buildings of his own erection, and to better the position of his industrious tenants, by rendering the size of their farms proportionate to their capital and energies, no law should impede his action, even though the operation involve the occasional conversion of a struggling tenant into a well-paid labourer or prosperous emigrant. Far from considering the latter alternative a hardship, I have invariably counselled emigration to any healthy single young man among my tenants in whom I was specially interested, and whose embarrass-ments at home compromised his future. In doing so I recommended the course I myself should have adopted under similar circumstances, and in no instance has the step been regretted. At this moment several of the most prosperous farmers on my estate are men who went out in their youth to Australia and to America, and have returned in the prime of life with an ample supply of capital, to renew with myself on a still more permanent basis the connexion which had subsisted for many generations between our respective ancestors."

It may be justly urged, that the moral character of an act of evic-tion will greatly depend on the complete termination of the tenant's legitimate interest in his farm ; but the argument presupposes this essential condition ; and when it is remembered that according to Judge Longfield's dictum " no improvement on a small farm will pay ; that there is no small portion of the land of Ireland in the hands of tenants to whom a promise of compensation for *bonâ fide* improvements would be useless: they have neither skill, capital, nor energy to undertake such tasks," and that the deterioration of the land, if justly estimated, would be found to outweigh, in most cases of eviction, the counter-claim of the tenant for compensation, it is improbable that many instances have occurred in which this condition has not been fulfilled. Therefore, while we freely admit that a heavy obligation rests upon the landlord to exercise such extreme rights with great moderation, and with a charity far in excess of his legal responsibilities, in the face of the foregoing considerations, it may well be doubted that it would be either just or wise to curtail them.

In fact, the transition which is affecting the agricultural world of Ireland resembles the revolution which overturned the manufacturing system of England on the introduction of the power-loom. In each case an improvement of method threw a large proportion of the population of either country out of their accustomed groove, and great suffering and discontent ensued; but, for Parliament or public opinion to compel the agricultural interest of Ireland to maintain an unprofitable or exploded system of husbandry, for the purpose of preventing emigration, would be as unreasonable as an edict to preclude the mill-owner of Manchester from adopting such mechanical improvements as economize manual labour, or from working half-time during a cotton famine.

That a moral duty rests on the promoters of every industry, whether commercial or agricultural, to mitigate the distress incident to those periods of transition which periodically disturb all branches of employment, cannot be too strongly insisted upon; but there can be no such essential difference in the relations between a landlord and his tenants, and an employer of wages and his workmen, *on the expiration of their respective contracts*, as should render such obligations more imperative on the one than on the other. Indeed, if a distinction were to be drawn, it would tell rather in the landlord's favour, inasmuch as the wealth accruing to him from the exertions of his tenants chiefly represents a low rate of interest on capital already accumulated without their co-operation; whereas, in the case of the manufacturer, a great portion of his capital, and of its rapidly increasing profits, has been created by the toil of those whom he finds it convenient to dismiss at a week's notice.

But, whatever the nature of the moral duties of landlord or master, under such circumstances, it is clear they cannot become the subject of legal enactment; and if any proof were needed of the ripeness of the working classes for a large extension of the franchise, it might be found in the economical sagacity and keen moral sense which have enabled them to distinguish the limits within which Parliament can be justly required to arbitrate in such matters between themselves and their employers.

Let us now turn to the two concluding points in our inquiry, viz.—1st, the extent to which the present discontent is to be attributed to laws affecting the tenure of land; and 2nd, the degree to which any change in those laws would modify that discontent. The existence of a certain amount of disaffection in the minds of a large section of the Irish race cannot be denied; but, in the first place, in defining its extent, we have the statements of the Catholic Prelates of Ireland, who have authoritatively pronounced it to be confined to the least respectable portion of the community, and, in the next, we must entirely dissociate it from the more subtle feeling of uneasiness which is said to pervade the minds of the tenant farmers of the south and west. What there is reason to dispute, is that the hostility manifested towards the Government of England by the Irish in America, in the great manufacturing towns of England and of Scotland, and by the non-occupying population of Ireland itself, has been occasioned by laws affecting the tenure of land, or is likely to be modified by any change in them.

Fixity of tenure would not have materially impeded the exodus after the potato famine, nor have affected the action of the landlords, in so far as they may have contributed to it; for even that fantastic desideratum—as advocated by Mr. Butt—presupposes good husbandry and the payment of rent; two conditions of which the great majority of the small occupiers who either left of their own accord or were evicted during these last five-and-twenty years were from the circumstances of the case incapable; so, even admitting that much of the ill-feeling of which Fenianism is the exponent is to be traced to the resentment of those who emigrated, it is clear that so long as the landlord is to be left with any control or proprietorship at all over his land, neither his conduct nor their opinion of it would have been materially modified. The same observation holds good even in a greater degree with respect to any law which might have regulated compensation, as the improvements on a cottier tenancy would have seldom been of an appreciable amount.* As a matter of fact, we believe that few of

* "Now the best friends of the Irish tenant must allow that there are fewer of the small land-holders who (in the sense that any tenant-right bill could recognize) have hitherto been improving tenants than there are of the reverse. Any legislation, therefore, that merely gave the tenant a property in his *bona fide* improvements could

the actual occupiers of land are tainted with Fenianism. Scarcely any farmers have been implicated in that conspiracy, though, perhaps, some of their relatives (in other words, persons with a much more modified interest in land than themselves) may have been entrapped. The tenant of a piece of land, even under the alleged disadvantageous condition of his existence, has much more to lose than to gain by the overthrow of the existing order of things. The adult male population of Ireland is about 1,900,000. Of these about 500,000 are the occupants of farms. In the event of a revolution the non-agricultural majority could alone hope to benefit by it. As political disturbances are unfavourable to the development of manufactures and the importation of capital, the population of Ireland would become more dependent upon the land than they are at present. It is true the landlord's rent would be at the disposal of the community; but, as it is but a fourth of the produce, its confiscation would only make room for about 100,000 new occupiers, without improving the condition of the present ones. But there will remain above a million of more or less necessitous persons to be accommodated, among whom, therefore, large sections of the present holdings would have to be divided, and filibustering patriots from America* might prove as exacting as Cromwell's troopers. But, though the farming classes of Ireland regard Fenianism with hostility and terror, it cannot be denied that in many districts they are restless and dissatisfied with their own position. The degree of this discontent is dependent upon different circumstances. Nowhere in Great Britain does there exist a more orderly or contented body of men than the tenantry of Ulster; and I believe that, so far from regarding what are called " the tenant-right agitators" with favour, they rather shrink from the risk of reducing the gracious customs which are now voluntarily maintained between them and their landlords into the definite and inelastic phraseology of the most liberal Tenants' Compensation Bill which could be devised.

be a boon at the present moment only to the minority of the tenant class. The larger number of the cottiers and small farmers, not having made any improvements, would be unaffected by the protecting law, and would be as liable as ever to unrecompensed eviction."—*Home and Foreign Review, April,* 1864, p. 353.

* A tenant in the South of Ireland lately received a letter from America, warning him at his peril to break up some pasture, as the writer intended on his arrival to appropriate the farm, of which it formed a part, himself. Were the American-Irish invasion ever to take place, the traditional claim which might be set up by the sons of a former generation of emigrants to portions of existing holdings might prove very embarrassing to their present occupants.

In the south and west matters are very different; but even there great diversity of sentiment exists; the aspirations of the peasantry being apt to take a local colouring, varying with the influences which have been brought to bear upon them—differing on different estates and in different counties, in some districts their utmost pretensions being most reasonable, while in others they are such as no legislation could satisfy; nor, unhappily, does it always follow that those tenants are the most contented who are treated with the greatest indulgence. But, though embodied in a hundred different modes of expression, the disquietude of the Irish occupier may be referred to three distinct conditions of thought:—First, a fear of any change in his position acting on a mind possessed with a blind, unreasoning hankering after a bit of land; the traditional failing of a people to whom for centuries land has been the only means of support, and which leaves them the moment they are surrounded by other associations. Secondly, a vague jealousy springing from his incapacity to understand the laws which regulate investments of capital in civilized countries, which makes the tenant grudge any expenditure on his farm that will be of ulterior benefit to his landlord, though it might in the meantime repay himself, capital and interest, twenty-fold. And thirdly, the legitimate anxiety of a thoughtful man, whose prospects are kept in perpetual hazard by his landlord's unwillingness or inability to grant an appropriate lease. Of these three separate causes of discord between the landlords and their tenants the two first are by far the most prolific of ill-feeling, and at the same time the most difficult to remove, and are aggravated not a little by selfish and unprincipled agitators.

The third cause—and, at the same time, the least prevailing—arises more frequently from the inability than from the unwillingness of the landlord. There are few proprietors who do not feel—and this feeling is increasing—that it is their interest to make a solvent, industrious, and intelligent tenant secure in his tenure, and contented with his position.* The readiness with which leases are granted to Scotch and English farmers, who are willing (if permitted by the people) to invest their capital on Irish soil, is a strong proof of this.

* Sir John Gray admits this in his speech at Manchester, October 18th, 1869. "The majority of landlords in Ireland," he says, "act in accordance with this principle (the right of occupancy at a full and fair rent), because they feel it to be beneficial to themselves and just to their tenants."

CHAPTER V.

PROPOSED REMEDIES IN THE LAND TENURE CONSIDERED.

THOSE various plans which have been proposed for the settlement of what is called " the Irish Land Question" may be grouped under four distinct methods of procedure. Let us consider in turn.

First in order comes the scheme (advocated by Mr. Bright), of enabling the peasantry of Ireland to buy up, with money advanced by Government, the estates of British noblemen happening to be owners of property in both countries, at a price 10 per cent. in excess of their value. Now, it would ill become Irish landlords to allude to such a proposal in any terms but those of respect and gratitude, as a genuine proof of the author's goodwill towards them. Nor do we dissent from Mr. Bright in regretting that so much of the land in Ireland should be possessed by those whose permanent home is never likely to be in that country, although the selection of names by which his well-meant suggestion was disfigured happened to be unfortunate. Had he contented himself with expressing a hope that it might be found convenient to some of the gentlemen circumstanced as he described, to allow their Irish property to descend (where family settlements would permit) in the line of their second sons—a suggestion already made by Mr. O'Connell—many would have cordially agreed with him, especially as the fact of estates having been in the course of sale at the rate of £1,000,000 a year in the Landed Estates' Court renders his offer of a premium unnecessary.

With regard to the eventual result of Mr. Bright's scheme on the happiness of the people, we may well entertain grave doubts. In the first place, the practical difficulties in the way of its execution would be enormous:—unless land is let much lower than Mr. Bright would probably care to admit, there are not many tenants who could afford to pay, in addition to their usual obligations, 5 or 6 per cent., for a number of years, on whatever sum the fee-simple of their holdings might be worth; and, in the next—until the operation was completed, Government would find itself charged with the responsibilities of a land agency of a most onerous character, over property scattered in innumerable small subdivisions up and down the country. Occasions would arise when the increased rent would cease to be forthcoming, and, as trustees for the tax-payer, the State would have to proceed against the defaulting tenant with inflexible rigour to resume possession of his holding—probably much deteriorated by necessitous husbandry—and either to confiscate the paid-up portion of the purchase money, which would be considered a gross injustice by the person evicted, or to return it to him, which would be an equally sensible loss to the Exchequer. But, supposing the creation of these small proprietorships happily effected, is it so certain that the general condition of the country would be improved? What guarantee have we against these several infinitesimal estates acquiring the character of the already existing perpetuities?* It is the fashion to argue that the relation of landlord and tenant, as it exists in England, cannot be comprehended by the genius of the Irish people. But it is the only relation the Irish peasant does (at least so long as he remains in Ireland) thoroughly appreciate. The labourer's dream is to become a tenant; the tenant's greatest ambition is to enjoy the dignity of a landlord. What he cannot be made to realize is, that an independent labourer is a more respectable personage than a struggling farmer, and a prosperous husbandman than a rack-renting squireen. It is true, were Mr. Bright's scheme to be put in operation, it would be perfectly justifiable for the State, while in promoting these purchases with public money, to impose stringent conditions against subletting; but such precautions would be found practically inoperative, or only to be enforced by a code of primogeniture, entail, and limited ownership, such as would keenly shock the advocates of the change, and would run counter to one of the most inveterate and favourite habits of Irish tenants—that of providing for children and their descendants by subdivision of their farms, a fact upon which we have already observed, and which is established by a host of witnesses before the Devon Commission, of different classes of politics, including Mr. O'Connell. Supposing, however, the system worked no worse in Ireland than in France, the state of agriculture in France, with so many advantages of climate and with such variety of resource, is not a re-assuring precedent.†

* Mr. Mill, with his usual sagacity, has detected the difficulties which might arise out of the indiscriminate conversion of the present tenantry into peasant-proprietors.

"A large proportion, also, of the present holdings are probably still too small to try the proprietary system under the greatest advantages ; nor are the tenants always the persons one would desire to select as the first occupants of peasant-properties."—*Mill's Polit. Econ.*, p. 411.

† Making every allowance for the improvement which has undoubtedly taken place of late years in French farming, it is still a considerable way behind England

"At this moment," says Lord Dufferin, in 1867, "I believe there are several hundred thousand small freeholders in that country too indigent to contribute their penny or half-penny a year to the taxation of the country. An excessive proportion of arable land lies fallow; the gross produce per acre is much less than it is in Belgium and England; a large number of their Liliputian estates are grievously encumbered; of some the original purchase money has not been paid; while Mr. Michelet has declared the position of the small French proprietor to be so intolerable, that the only hope of salvation for the agricultural interest of France lies in the repudiation of all mortgages."

If, then, competition, generated by a very minute subdivision of landed property, has produced these results in France, where the rural population scarcely increases, and where there exists a large manufacturing industry to absorb the surplus labour of the agricultural districts, its effect in Ireland might be yet more disastrous. Therefore, though heartily sympathizing with Mr. Bright in his desire to see a substantial yeoman class established in Ireland, and admitting that to many individual cases the objections indicated would not apply, we fear the comprehensive scheme by which he proposes to attain that object, is not sufficiently promising to justify us in running the risk it would entail.

We now come to a series of proposals of a very different complexion, proposals which involve the transfer of a large amount of proprietary rights from the landlord to the tenant. We do not deny the right of the State in cases of emergency to deal in a very peremptory manner with private property of all kinds, and especially with landed property; but, in assuming this right, it must be made clear that its exercise will be of indisputable benefit to the community at large, and the individual to whose prejudice it is enforced must be compensated at the public expense to the

and Belgium, and whatever progress is being made is rather in spite than in consequence of the extreme comminution of the soil Even Mr. Mill admits the tendency to subdivision in France has been too great, though the cultivation of the vine is so peculiarly adapted to "la petite culture." Native authors visit it with more serious reprobation.

"1 know that ten years' produce per acre in France, as a whole (though not in its most improved districts), averages much less than in England."—*Mill's Polit. Econ.*, p. 189.

"Undue subdivision, and excessive smallness of holdings, are undoubtedly a prevalent evil in some countries of peasant proprietors, and particularly in parts of Germany and France."

"The Governments of Bavaria and Nassau have thought it necessary to impose a legal limit to subdivision, and the Prussian Government unsuccessfully proposed the same measure to the Estates of its Rhenish Provinces."—*Dig. Dev. Com.*, p. 381.

full amount of the injury he sustains.* The safety of a nation may depend upon the security of an arsenal, and that of the arsenal on the conversion of a hovel into a redoubt; yet the engineer in command dare no more remove a brick from the obnoxious premises without the sanction of an Act of Parliament, and an elaborate valuation, than he dare blow up St. Paul's.

But considerations such as these, the authors of the various schemes " for dealing vigorously with the Irish landlords" deem beneath their notice.

The most notable plan is one lately promulgated by Mr. Butt, a gentleman of eminence in his profession. As his plan is typical of a large series of others, it may be well to examine it. It is embodied in the form of a projected Act of Parliament, which declares that after the said Act every tenant who chooses to claim its protection shall be entitled to a lease of 63 years at a rent one-third below the full or competition value. Thus, by a single stroke of the pen, the whole of the landed property of Ireland is to be withdrawn from the control and enjoyment of those who have either purchased or inherited it, and is to remain for two entire generations at the disposal of the 540,000 persons who may happen at the time of the passing of the Act to be in the occupation of its several sub-divisions. This, too, without reference to their individual qualifications, and in the teeth of the condemnation passed by the tenants' best friends on even a 21 years' lease, if granted for a holding of less than 15 acres, within which category more than one-third of the farms of Ireland still remain.

* Even Mr. Mill, though inspired with no very indulgent feelings towards the landlords of Ireland, admits this principle.

"The claim of the landowners to the land is altogether subordinate to the general policy of the State. The principle of property gives them no right to the land, but only a right to compensation for whatever portion of their interest in the land it may be the policy of the State to deprive them of. *To that, their claim is indefeasible.* It is due to landowners, and to owners of any property whatever, recognized as such by the State, that they should not be dispossessed of it without receiving its pecuniary value, or an annual income equal to what they derived from it. This is due on the general principles on which property rests. If the land was bought with the produce of the labour and abstinence of themselves or their ancestors, compensation is due to them on that ground; even if otherwise, it is still due on the ground of prescription. *When the property is of a kind to which peculiar affections attach themselves, the compensation ought to exceed a bare pecuniary equivalent.* The legislature, which if it pleased might convert the whole body of landlords into fundholders or pensioners, might, *à fortiori*, commute the average receipts of Irish landlords into a fixed rent charge, and raise the tenants into proprietors; supposing always that the full market value of the land was tendered to the landlords, in case they preferred that to accepting the conditions proposed."—*Mill, Polit. Econ.*, p. 289.

Let us now look more narrowly into the operation of this plan. Every Irishman will probably judge of it as it affects himself. Let us hear Lord Dufferin upon this view of the subject, the rather as his case is that of many others whose properties lie in the neighbourhood of towns on the lines of railways on the sea coast and in other rising localities:—

"I possess," he says,* "a strip of some three or four hundred acres, bordering the Lough of Belfast, peculiarly suitable for villas. I have been offered from £15 to £20 an acre for a portion of this land (most of which I have inherited from an ancestor who made his fortune as a merchant, and part of which I have recently purchased with the proceeds of the sale of some English property). A railway along the shore still further increases its attractions, and at a particular point there is a sandy bay which—as the site of a bathing village—may eventually become a favourite resort for the inhabitants of Belfast. For various reasons I have hitherto deferred leasing any of the land, and it is at present in the occupation of agricultural tenants, all of whom have been for many years in the enjoyment of beneficial leases, which have either expired or will shortly do so. We will suppose that Mr. Butt's Bill passes; the accidental occupants of this property become tenants for another additional term of 63 years; I am unexpectedly precluded from applying my land to its most remunerative use; and a project which would have diffused the wealth of a rich community over a large agricultural area is indefinitely postponed—unless, indeed, I choose to buy back my own property, at a price, probably, not much lower than the original value of the fee simple, from tenants who have neither legal nor equitable claims against me.† Moreover it is to be remembered that the circumstances I have detailed are not exceptional, but prevail more or less in the vicinity of every large town; that there is no district which may not, at one time or another, be affected by analogous influences, and that it is its very susceptibility of a rise in price that contributes an important element to the value of landed property, and reconciles the purchaser to the low rate of interest proximately derived from it."

But let us regard Mr. Butt's proposal from another point of view. Probably, if asked for a justification of his measures, he would allege the right of the tenant to the enjoyment of his "improvements." Let us concede this right. But how about the

* *Irish Emigration*, 2nd Ed., p. 229.

"† This instance is rendered the more striking by the fact that I am paying £9 an acre per annum, i.e., its market price, as building ground, for part of the land for which my agricultural tenants are only paying me 30s. By Mr. Butt's Bill both arrangements would be made equally permanent.

improvements which have not been made by the tenant, or which have been bought up by the landlord, or which though effected by the tenant have been executed under express contracts, and in consideration of reduced rents or long leases no uncommon case, especially on unreclaimed lands? By what canon of justice does he expropriate these? Surely, if a tenant have an equitable claim for compensation, or to extension of occupancy in lieu of compensation, for money he imprudently risked on the prospective chance of his landlord's liberality, the landlord himself has a right to be continued in possession of that to which his equitable claim is as good, and his legal right so much better!

But it will be said, " the improvements on farms in Ireland are invariably made by the tenants." In a great number of instances this is the case. But the reverse is far more frequent than is generally supposed. Judge Longfield has stated that almost all the larger drainage works, and a considerable proportion even of the minor improvements, have been executed by the proprietors. We know from official returns that within eighteen years more than £1,800,000 of borrowed money has been sunk by them in draining and building alone. This sum is no test, however, of what they have expended besides out of their incomes. The Devon Commission reported that on twenty-two estates (many of them the largest in the country), the buildings had been erected at the sole expense of the landlord. But this statement does not imply that there were not other properties on which the same rule prevailed. Only a certain number of estates were brought under their notice. In many cases not noticed great exertions have been made by the landlords, and on numerous estates in various parts of the country sums varying from £30,000 to £40,000 have been expended on farm-steadings and cottages during the last fifty years.

" I myself," continues Lord Dufferin, " have spent £10,000 in buying up the improvements of my tenants, besides what I have sunk in executing new ones. Many of my neighbours are doing the same, and every year our efforts in this direction are likely to extend, unless, indeed, Mr. Butt's ingenious device for proving the superior discretion of keeping our money in our pockets should suddenly put a stop to the process."

Having glanced at the probable wrong to the landlord, let us estimate the degree to which the tenant would be benefited. Leases are undoubtedly favourable to agriculture, and an advantage to the tenant. But as to the terms of tenure, there is a great diversity of opinion. Judge Longfield condemns long leases; nor was the state of Ireland 40 years ago a very satisfactory proof of their efficiency. In Belgium three, five, and nine years are the accepted terms; in Scotland, 13 and 19; in England, 21. By what statistical canon does Mr. Butt arbitrarily extend them to 63! We have already seen the fervent advocates of the leasing system deprecate the extension of leases to such small areas as 15 acres; others of even greater experience, and no less friendly to the tenant, have raised the minimum to 30, 40, 50 acres. Even Mr. Bright takes a man paying £50 of rent as his typical yeoman. In the face of these opinions why should any one seek to stereotype a condition of affairs confessedly detrimental to the interests of agriculture? One of the greatest benefits to Ireland has resulted from the legal machinery invented to transfer the estates of incumbered proprietors to the hands of persons with sufficient capital to improve them. Surely the same policy ought to be pursued in facilitating the transference of farms from the impoverished agriculturist to the man of energy and capital? Yet Mr. Butt, like the malevolent fairy in the tale of the " Sleeping Beauty," would curse with the doom of rigid immobility for the greater portion of a century, without the prospect of that magic " after-glow" of renewed life and vigour which completes the story.

Again, though this is his intention, the means he adopts would lead to another result. With a fatal ingenuity he contrives to make it the imperative interest of the landlords to get rid of their tenants, and at the same time furnishes them with ample facilities for the process. He plucks the lion's beard with one hand, and whets his fangs and talons with the other. If the landlord is precluded by law from letting his land except on disadvantageous terms, he will naturally prefer to keep it in his own hands. Bad husbandry and non-payment of rent, and neglect of improvements, constitute, even according to Mr. Butt, just occasions of eviction, which he proposes to be absolute, and without redemption. By the inflexible application of these principles there is no property in Ireland which would not be cleared of a large proportion of its occupants in ten years, and the immediate effect of his beneficent efforts would be universal discontent and an enormous stimulus to emigration, counterbalanced perhaps by a rapid improvement in cultivation and a brevet promotion for some hundreds of thousands of agricultural labourers at the expense of a corresponding number of tenant farmers.

With regard to the minor principle involved in Mr. Butt's plan of fixing the rent of land by a Government officer, we need not trouble our readers. A moment's reflection will show how impossible it would be for any one but those immediately interested to arrive at a correct estimate of what particular areas could afford to pay. At this moment there are three standards of land valuation in Ireland,—there is the competition, or tenant's rent, which is generally in excess of what his limited skill and capital would enable him to pay; there is the agent's rent, which is regulated by what his experience tells him the tenant is able to pay without embarrassment; and there is the theoretical rent, which the land ought to pay if properly cultivated.* This latter rent would probably far exceed even the competition rent, yet no other one could be equitably adopted in any compulsory valuation. Judge Longfield has effectually illustrated the impracticability and injustice of any such system, based, as it is, upon a principle in direct antagonism to the conditions which usually regulate the relations betwixt man and man.

Before, however, dismissing from our attention these barren schemes for fixity of tenure, compulsory leases of greater or less

---

* Supposing that land which, if properly cultivated, would bear a rent of 40s. per acre, and for which the tenants themselves would offer 30s. at an auction (which, for the sake of argument, we will admit their want of skill and capital would render them incompetent to pay),—were valued by the Government officers at 20s., what would be the effect? Why that at the first devolution of the tenancy, the outgoing tenant or his representative would exact from the in-comer a fine exactly equivalent to so many years' purchase of the difference between the restricted rent of 20s. an acre, and the competition rent of 30s.: the effect of the transaction being that the new tenant would be charged with a double rent for all time to come, and that the landlord would have been defrauded of what, so far as it represents any value at all, is a portion of the fee simple of his estate. It is useless to object that the vigilance of the landlord could prevent so nefarious a transaction. The landlord in the first place is almost powerless to restrain these surreptitious arrangements, as any one who knows the north of Ireland is aware, and in the next place, he would have no particular interest in doing so. The sagacious legislation we are considering will have reduced the landlord to the position of a mere mortgagee, on what was once his property. Nothing that he can do, will either enhance or diminish its value. All personal relations between his tenantry and himself would be at an end, and his functions as a proprietor would be confined to issuing instruction to his solicitor to evict the moment his rent was a shilling in arrear. Whether the result would diminish or encourage landlords to live on their estates, we leave to the consideration of those who may be inclined to pursue the investigation further.

duration, and arbitrary rents, we would ask their authors and advocates whether it is altogether wise to persist in conjuring up before the imagination of ill-educated and impulsive men delusive expectations which can never be realized, and which, if realized, would only work their ruin. It is an easy task to persuade even the best-balanced minds that what appears to be for their interest is right; but to blunt the moral perceptions of ignorant men, to put evil for good, and good for evil, to sow dissension between those who should be friends, and to inaugurate a hopeless agitation in a country whose only chance of happiness is in peace and quiet—seems too sinister a mission to be excused by the perverted benevolence which inspires it.*

We now come to a very different group of propositions—propositions advocated by persons of gravity and authority, having for their object, not the confiscation of property, nor the curtailment of indefeasible rights; but the restoration to a more healthy condition of those relations between the owner and the occupier of land, which peculiar circumstances have invested with an abnormal character. If we cannot accept them as a resolution of our difficulties, it is not that we deny the existence of the evils they are intended to remedy, or that we fail to sympathize with the motives which have led to their suggestion.

The object proposed is the establishment of a conviction in the mind of every tenant in Ireland that if he invests his capital in the proper cultivation of his farm, either his occupation shall be sufficiently prolonged to enable him to reap the full reward of his industry, or, if abruptly terminated without his fault by his landlord, he shall receive a corresponding recompense in money. The claim embodied in the foregoing formula is obviously founded on the principles of natural justice. When a landlord hands over his field to the husbandman, even if there be no written agreement, a tacit understanding is implied that the man who sows shall reap; a contrary supposition would be adverse to public policy. Consequently, a law of emblements prevails in every civilized country. But, as the ulterior considerations of the bargain are susceptible of

---

* It may not be uninstructive to subjoin the late Mr. O'Connell's opinion of fixity of tenure.

"A more absurd and unjust plan he never heard of ; it did not do anything for the labourer of the country, it transferred the fee-simple from the present proprietor to the present occupier of large farms ; it was in fact creating a smaller monopoly than the former one, but equally mischievous in its nature."

every variety of arrangement, they have been left by the common consent of mankind to be regulated by contract, in whatever manner may suit the convenience of the parties interested. It is urged, however, that in Ireland the dependence of the population upon agriculture is so complete that competition has destroyed the tenant's freedom of action. He has been driven into a bargain so inequitable as would justify the state in substituting for the conditions he himself is eager to accept such an extension of the principle out of which has originated the law of emblements as shall secure to him the fruits of his investments—whether in the larger operations of husbandry, or in the erection of the farm buildings they require. But it is to be observed that this plea of the helpless position of the tenant, whatever force it might have had, is no longer valid, inasmuch as the alternative of adequate wages is now open to him; that the reckless acquisition of land, to which often he cannot do justice, is the result of a passion to be discouraged rather than stimulated; and that the same considerations which would justify the State in regulating the incidental conditions of occupancy, would also entitle it to fix the remuneration of labour; it is doubtful, therefore, whether any circumstances would render it advisable for Government to depart from the rule which experience has taught us to be best in the long run—viz., to leave the rights of contract between individuals as free as possible.

This conclusion acquires greater force, when we consider how objectionable are the means which even the most sagacious minds have suggested for the application of a contrary principle—such, for instance, as the extension to the tenant of a legal right, first, to make what he may call an "improvement" against the express wish of his landlord, and then to claim compensation for it. Now the very essence of the law of emblements is, that the operation for which compensation is claimed should be of indisputable advantage to the landlord's property. Ploughing, seeding, and manuring fulfil these conditions. But the best method of conducting the more complex operations of husbandry, not even excluding draining, and certainly including the erection of farm-buildings, is often a matter of dispute between high authorities; and a tenant may embark in an expenditure which, though not exactly disadvantageous to his farm, may be very detrimental to the estate of which his farm is part. Judge Longfield himself tells us that "no improvement on a small farm will pay," and gives good reasons for his opinion, consequently such improvements, if they are made at all, should be made at the tenant's own risk, and not at the risk of the person who objects to them. It is urged that the quality of the intended improvement might be decided by some impartial tribunal; but should the owner of a property be convinced that a particular operation would damage rather than benefit his estate— would interfere with his own schemes of improvement, would load, for instance, with useless agricultural erections, lands he contemplated devoting to building purposes—it would be unjust to allow an assistant barrister (even though instructed by a *comitatus* of experts) to override his decision. This would be felt so keenly— that, should a tenant be found commencing an "improvement" against which his landlord had protested, he would invariably receive notice to quit. We fear, therefore, we must reject this principle, as both unjust and impracticable. .

We now come to the proposal made by the Government—a proposal dictated by an anxious desire to make as large a concession as possible to the equitable claims of the tenant, and which—with a moderation that did them honour—was accepted, we believe, by the most distinguished of the Liberal members for Ireland, as a settlement of the question. The essence of the arrangement was, to leave the right of contract perfectly free; but to substitute, where no contract existed, a presumption that, within certain limits, any improvement made by the tenant was his property. That such a declaration on the part of the law is no interference with the right of property, cannot be disputed, and it is in some such compromise, if in any, a solution of the Irish land question is to be found.

The wisdom of Parliament would, probably, have simplified the details of the measure. It may fairly be urged that the safeguards introduced for the protection of the landlord, only confused the principle of the bill. Instead of limiting the tenant's claim for compensation, on account of an uncovenanted improvement, to a maximum of £5 per acre, it would be better to leave him entirely unrestricted in his expenditure. Instead of declaring his ownership in that improvement to be annihilated at the expiration of an arbitrary period, the law should presume it to endure as long as the beneficial effects of its operation lasted. Instead of attempting to regulate the relations of the two parties by the ambiguous provisions of a fictitious lease, it would be simpler to reverse to a certain extent the existing presumption of law, that whatever is affixed to the soil belongs to the landlord, and to declare instead, that any *bonâ fide* improvement, executed by a tenant, outside of a written

contract, is the property of the tenant, for which, on surrendering
possession of his farm, whether of his own accord or under compulsion, he shall be entitled to receive compensation from his landlord
to the amount of the additional value annually accruing from it, to
be assessed by arbitration, or recovered in a court of law. It may
be objected that such a method of procedure involves an inequitable
principle of compensation, and prejudices the interests of the landlord. That may be admitted. But it has been already stated that
a tenant's *equitable* claim to compensation should be regulated by
the original cost of the improvement, and the rate of interest due
to such investments,* but in declaring a presumption *in the absence
of a contract*, the law does not pretend to lay down a canon of
equity, and the change would be only unfair to the landlord to the
same degree and in the same sense as the converse is now unfair to
to the tenant.

Under the existing statute, if a yearly occupier of a farm
expends £500 in the erection of a house, the law *presumes* the
building to belong to the owner of the soil, and he might claim
possession the day after it was built. For the law to declare its
value to be the property of the tenant as long as that value
endures would be even a less extravagant presumption. It was
never contemplated, however, that a naked presumption of this
kind should regulate the ultimate arrangement; but as, in the
absence of any specific agreement on the subject, it was necessary
to attribute the property to some one, it was naturally assigned to
the person with whose estate it had become irrevocably incorporated, in the expectation that the original presumption created
by the law would be expressly confirmed, modified, or reversed by
a subsequent agreement framed in accordance with the interests of
the contracting parties. Unhappily, in Ireland this expectation
has been frustrated. Those very persons to whom the unmitigated
application of this legal presumption would be most injurious,
have been often too careless—sometimes too confiding—too
dependent—to adopt the countervailing precautions which, in
other countries, the prudence of mankind has rendered universal.
As a consequence, the untempered presumption of the law acts
occasionally in Ireland with a severity it was never intended
should attach to it. Let us then change that presumption, and
impose upon those who are in a better position to do so, the

* Judge Longfield is very explicit on this point. See his Evidence, and that of
Mr. Curling to the same effect before the Devon Commission.

obligation of protecting themselves from whatever consequences its unqualified application would entail; since the tenants will not insist upon defining their rights by specific agreements, let us make it the interest of the landlords to do so, and as it is the practice in many parts of Ireland for the tenant to execute a considerable proportion of the improvement, let us bring the presumption of the law more into harmony with such practice. By this means a constant statutory bias would be brought to bear in favour of the tenant; he would obtain immunity from the consequences of his own carelessness, and he would invariably profit by the carelessness of his landlord; while, at the same time, the latter would have it in his power to correct the partiality of the law by the provisions of an equitable contract.

But if this much is conceded to the peculiar position to which subdivision, competition, and an inordinate desire to possess land has reduced the Irish tenant, it would be advisable, both in the interest of the tenant himself and of the landlord, to accompany the foregoing alteration of the law by some subsidiary provision for the registration of every improvement on which it is intended to found a claim for compensation. The necessity for such a precaution is self-evident. Without it no Court would possess trustworthy data for estimating the nature and cost of an alleged improvement made ten or fifteen years before the inquiry into its title to compensation was instituted. Were such matters to be left to oral evidence, and to the recollection of the individuals interested, a satisfactory settlement could never be attained. A single exemplification will suffice. Perhaps there is no improvement more common, more deserving of compensation, or requiring a longer term of occupancy to repay itself, than that which consists in quarrying, and in removing or burying the rocks which crop up in a shallow and stony soil; yet the very perfection of the operation destroys all internal evidence of what has been done. The tenant's claim will therefore have to rest on testimony. But long before any question of compensation comes to be raised, the author of the improvement may have died, or he may have handed over his interest in his farm to another man. The estate itself may have been sold, and a new agent and a new landlord have come upon the scene. Yet though all the parties privy to the original arrangement have disappeared, the claim itself would be as rife as ever. How is the matter to be adjudicated in the absence of competent witnesses or trustworthy data? And it is to be

E

remembered that the difficulty of adjusting *bonâ fide* claims of this description, is the true measure of the facilities which would be afforded for establishing unsubstantial and fraudulent pretensions on venal evidence.

Again, if tenants are to be entitled to get back from their landlord whatever they may choose to lay out on their farms, it is essential that the latter should have the means of acquainting himself with the bill which is being run up against him on various parts of his estate. No one would allow the most trustworthy steward to embark in an unlimited expenditure on his home-farm without looking occasionally at his books; still less would it be advisable to allow a numerous tenantry to incur, on behalf of their landlord, an unknown amount of responsibilities which, however insignificant in each instance, would, in the aggregate, amount to an enormous sum. In some parts of Ireland as many as 4,000 or 5,000 tenants are located on a single property; and it must be recollected that frequently they have become thus numerous, not through the landlord's neglect, but by the evasion of express covenants against sub-letting. Supposing each tenant to spend £10 a year in some alleged improvement,—the straightening of a fence, the repair of a gable end, the erection of a pig-stye—at the end of five years the owner of such a property might find himself confronted by a claim to compensation amounting to £200.000. With this contingency in prospect, but without any means of ascertaining the rate at which the burden was accumulating, the landowner would be in a position of such insecurity as would compel him either to reduce his tenantry to more manageable proportions, or else to emasculate their claims by imposing a specific agreement on each tenant to execute *seriatim* every agricultural operation of which his farm was susceptible. It is argued that the very fact of warning the landlord of what was taking place on his estate would tend to discountenance the tenant's improvements. Such an objection can hardly be seriously urged. Under any circumstances an improvement hatched like a conspiracy, and exploded like a mine would probably lead to the improver being hoisted with his own petard.

Lastly, it is the interest of the tenantry, even more than that of their landlords, that the investment of capital in improvements should be effected with care and economy, and kept at a *minimum*, as the burden of compensation invariably falls on the incoming tenant. This point was very distinctly noted in the report of Mr. Pusey's Parliamentary Committee; and it is evident that, if a landlord is to pay a certain sum to an outgoing tenant for his improvements, he will recoup himself, either by clapping an equivalent percentage on the rent of the new tenant, or by accepting a fine equivalent in amount to the sum he has paid away. To stimulate an unnecessary expenditure on any estate, whether in the shape of superfluous farm buildings or other so-called improvements, is only to embarrass the community located upon it with a burden as irredeemable as a national debt. Yet no surer way to encourage such extravagance can be devised than to allow one set of men to disburse without restraint or inquiry sums of money which they expect another set of men will have to repay. The possibility of the claim being eventually disallowed would be too remote a contingency to influence their conduct, while the chance of the award being in excess of their expenditure would still further neutralize their prudence.

Stripped, however, of the complicated provisions which confused and indeed altered the original principle it professed to enunciate, the Bill of the Government certainly contained the germ of what might prove both a politic and legitimate measure. As to any further or more intimate interference by the legislature between landlord and tenant we cannot be sanguine. Some persons would prefer to create by Act of Parliament a model lease, and then to render the position of any landlord who might decline to adopt it so untenable as to impose on him, if not a legal obligation, at all events an imperative necessity to bring the tenures on his estate into conformity with its provisions. Now, however strong an advocate for leases one may be, even though he considers that to refuse a lease to a solvent industrious tenant is little short of a crime, and that the prosperity of agriculture depends on security of tenure, and that the only proper tenure is a liberal lease. Yet one cannot conceive, we think, a measure more fraught with disaster to agriculture, more productive of discontent, more certain to inflict suffering on a large proportion of the present tenant farmers of the country, than that the Irish landlords should be driven by any such legislation as this into an indiscriminate issue of leases for a term of years.

None but persons acquainted with the management of Irish property can have an adequate idea of the variety of instances in which it may become inexpedient to grant a lease. Very

68

frequently, particularly in the North of Ireland, the tenantry unfortunately prefer an indefinite understanding to a specific contract. It is doubtful whether, even in the South, leases for anything but an unreasonable period would be considered as a boon, and they have often been declined on account of the expense. Yet to force a lease on an unwilling tenant is only a degree less objectionable than to evict him for refusing to take one. In many instances, the only reason for which a lease is desired, is to obtain a document on which money can be raised, or an extravagant charge for younger children effected. If, therefore, some of the landed proprietors of Ireland evince a disinclination to grant leases, it is, in many instances, because bitter experience has taught them that previous leases have generally proved to be, as Judge Longfield has observed, "all in the tenant's favour"—that a certain proportion of their actual tenants are incapable of fulfilling the obligations of a contract—that security of tenure,—in other words, immunity from all sense of responsibility,—instead of stimulating the industry of the occupier, too often acts as a premium on idleness, and that the difficulties of preventing the subdivision and subletting of leased lands, are almost insurmountable. The case of a solvent and improving tenant being refused a lease, is, we suspect, much rarer than is supposed.

The consequences of forcing leases by Act of Parliament are sufficiently obvious. Hitherto, one of the chief accusations brought against the Irish proprietor has been his indifference to the character and the solvency of his tenant, and in order to correct this indifference it is proposed to abolish the priority of his claim on the rent, and to reduce him to the ranks of an ordinary creditor. If, therefore, under these circumstances he is precluded from letting his land, except under a thirty one years' lease, an inexorable necessity will be imposed upon him to exclude from such a permanent arrangement those of his existing tenants who are in debt, or who are likely to fall into embarrassment during the obligatory term. Lord Dufferin justly observes:—

"Perhaps the tenantry of no estate in Ireland is more prosperous than my own ; yet my agent informs me that, unhappily, more than a third of the farmers upon my property are under heavy pecuniary obligations through the country, in addition to those incurred towards myself. At present their creditors are aware that to drive them from their farms by the application of any premature pressure would only reduce to a minimum their own chances of receiving payment. My own inclination is to give them every opportunity to extricate themselves from their difficulties ; and though the position of affairs is not satisfactory, nor can the ultimate destiny of many of these persons be doubtful, a reasonable amount of forbearance on my part may save some, and greatly mitigate the hardship of their situation to the rest.

" If, however, I found myself suddenly called upon by Parliament to lease away my estates for a whole generation, matters would be brought to a crisis, and in self-defence I should be forced (very much against my will) to exclude from the intended benefits of the arrangement every single individual circumstanced as I have described. No landlord could be expected to grant a lease to a bankrupt, or to enter into a contract with a person incapable of fulfilling its obligations.

" But, in addition to those of my tenants who are actually in debt, there are a certain number who are so destitute of capital—so unskilful —occupiers of such small and inconvenient patches—so near the verge of ruin—as to be very unfit recipients of a lease. However willing I might be to continue them in their present holdings until an opportunity shall occur of establishing them as labourers, or of enabling their sons to emigrate, or of converting the old people into pensioners, a very different arrangement would be necessary if Parliament held a pistol to my head, and left me no choice but to give them 31 years' leases, or resume possession of my land. Now if these undesirable contingencies might arise on a prosperous estate in Ulster, it is scarcely necessary to indicate what would be the consequences of such anomalous interference by Parliament in the south and west of Ireland."

Take the case of the falling in of an old 61 years' lease, on which, in spite of all covenants to the contrary, a vast congeries of cottier tenants have been collecting for generations. Perhaps the size of the holdings may not average four acres a piece: a great deal of it may be held in rundale: all of it is sure to be in the worst possible condition; yet the only chance of introducing a better system—of inducing the people to agglomerate their patches —of making arrangements for the squaring up of fields, and the re-distribution of the area into a shape more suitable to existing circumstances—is that the landlord should have some power of controlling the ignorant prejudices of those for whose well-being he has become suddenly responsible. Under any circumstances the task will require patience—above all—time; five, ten, fifteen years, perhaps a lifetime will be necessary if the operation is to be performed with due regard to the feelings of the people concerned. But if the landlord be peremptorily required to re-lease his land for another generation, any such benevolent construction will be impossible, and the only alternative left to him will be to re-stereotype the existing chaos, or to convert his estate into a *tabula-rasa.*

In fact, the more the matter is considered the greater are the difficulties which present themselves. Unless great care is taken we shall injure rather than improve the position of our clients. As long as a numerous population is cursed with a morbid craving to possess land, so long will the owner of land be able to drive hard bargains in spite of Queen, Lords, and Commons, and any exceptional legislation we may devise will be more apt effectually to embarrass the judicious management of the liberal landowner than it will control the injustice of the oppressor, while the ultimate result of our well meant endeavours may be to transfer the management of a great portion of every estate in Ireland from the hands of the land agent into those of the solicitor.

There is one further suggestion which might go far to diminish discontent and stimulate production amongst the agricultural class. In considering the question of tenants' improvements it is probable that a satisfactory settlement for the past is even a greater desideratum than the most favourable arrangement for the future. The legal attainment of this object has been given up by every one as imprac-ticable; yet if the people of England are really disposed to be as liberal as Mr. Bright's proposal implies, there is no reason why the same principle which has been introduced by Parliament to facilitate the future improvement of Ireland might not be adopted to obliterate all misunderstanding as to the past. No later than the Session of 1866 a million of money was voted to enable the owners of property in Ireland to erect farm buildings, and labourers' cottages, to drain and to reclaim. If a similar loan were granted on the same terms, or if the present loan were made accessible to those landlords who might be willing to buy up the existing improvements of their tenants, no doubt advantage would be taken of the opportu-nity. Precautions could be adopted by the Board of Works to ascertain that the improvements to be purchased were sufficient security for the sum borrowed. Though the landlord would be responsible for the debt, the interest on it would be repaid, either in whole or in part by the tenant. The tenant would be benefited by receiving a lump sum, which, if judiciously invested in his farm, would return him a profit of 3, 4, or 5 per cent. in excess of the yearly instalment for the discharge of the interest. It might be even advisable for the Board of Works to make these loans condi-tional on the occupier's receiving a lease.

By this simple expedient it would become the landlord's interest, not only to recognize the *minimum* claims of his tenant (which in many instances would become almost inappreciable beneath the strict scrutiny of a Court of Equity), but to deal with them in a liberal spirit; while both landlord and tenant would have an inducement to refer all matters in dispute between them to the arbitrament of a Board, in whose decision it would be the policy of each to acquiesce. A better understanding would be introduced between the two classes; even evictions would lose their most obnoxious characteristic; and, above all, a large sum of money now locked up in homesteads and farm buildings would be immediately transmuted into capital applicable to the cultivation of the soil.

It is impossible to lay too great stress on this last advantage. When people talk of *le petite culture*, and the reduplicated employment afforded by spade husbandry, they quite forget that, except in very favoured soils, low farming reduces land to a *caput mortuum*. All the labour in the world will not fertilize a sandbank; but convey to it the scourings of a great city, and a *minimum* of labour will turn it into a garden. Let capital overflow her soil,—an analogous transformation will take place in Ireland,—and though her superficial area remain the same, the stimulus to her powers of production would be equivalent to an accession of territory sufficient to support thousands in affluence, where at present hundreds find a difficulty in extracting a bare subsistence. Lord Dufferin says:—

"But it may be asked, Is this, then, all you have to propose? Have you no comprehensive remedy to prescribe for the perennial discontent of Ireland? Can no styptic be discovered for the unprecedented emigration from her shores? I answer that such inquiries lie beyond the scope of this hasty dissertation. I have never presumed to discuss the state of Ireland at large: but many persons having expressed an opinion that Irish disaffection, and the emigration from Ireland, were occasioned by the conduct of the landlords towards their tenants, and the iniquity of the laws affecting the tenure of land, I have ventured to examine the grounds on which those opinions are founded. The result has tended to show not only that no alteration of tenure would have an appreciable effect upon either, but that even the amendments I have indicated, however desirable in themselves, could have no very immediate effect on the evils we deplore. These evils are too deeply seated, too intimately interwoven with the past, to be cured by any empirical peddling in the land-laws of the country. To expect 'a tenant's compensation bill' to quell Fenianism, or to prevent those who cannot get a living at home from crossing the Atlantic, would be as reasonable as to try to stifle a conflagration on the first floor by stuffing a blanket down the kitchen chimney, or to staunch the haemorrhage from an artery by slipping the key of the house-door down your back. No nation can be made industrious, provident, and skilful, by Act of Parliament. It is to time, to education, and, above all, to the development of our industrial resources, that we must look for the reinvigoration of our economical constitution.

" I have now finished my ungracious task. To many I shall have appeared to take the part of the rich against the poor, of the strong against the weak, but to those who are practically acquainted with the subject it will be apparent that I have been arguing in the real interests of the latter, even more than in those of the former. If I am anxious to prevent the introduction of a vicious principle into the land-laws of Ireland, it is because I am convinced that the evil consequences of such mistaken legislation will fall again, as it has done before, on the tenant, rather than on the landlord. If I run counter to the instincts of that great Liberal party to whom Ireland owes so much, and from which it has still so much to expect, it is because I know its confidence has been abused. My only object has been to establish truth and to advocate justice. The doctrine that Ireland is to be saved by the sacrifice of the rights of property is a violation of both,—and its application would only aggravate our existing difficulties."

www.ingramcontent.com/pod-product-compliance
Lightning Source LLC
Chambersburg PA
CBHW020241090426
42735CB00010B/1792